Mid-Mississippi Regional Library System
3 6095 0021 6593 2

Melton, Brian C.,
Robert E. Lee :
36095002165932
MMRLS-WAL

D1173876

ROBERT E. LEE

Recent Titles in Greenwood Biographies

John F. Kennedy: A Biography
Michael Meagher and Larry D. Gragg

Maya Lin: A Biography
Donald Langmead

Stonewall Jackson: A Biography
Ethan S. Rafuse

Rosa Parks: A Biography
Joyce A. Hanson

Emiliano Zapata: A Biography
Albert Rolls

Diego Rivera: A Biography
Manuel Aguilar-Moreno and Erika Cabrera

Ronald Reagan: A Biography
J. David Woodard

Pancho Villa: A Biography
Alejandro Quintana

Michelle Obama: A Biography
Alma Halbert Bond

Lady Gaga: A Biography
Paula Johanson

Bono: A Biography
David Kootnikoff

Henry Louis Gates, Jr.: A Biography
Meg Greene

92
Lee

B&T
5-16-12

WB
37.00

ROBERT E. LEE

A Biography

Brian C. Melton

GREENWOOD BIOGRAPHIES

GREENWOOD

AN IMPRINT OF ABC-CLIO, LLC
Santa Barbara, California • Denver, Colorado • Oxford, England

Mid-Mississippi Regional Library System
Attala, Holmes, Leake, Montgomery
and Winston Counties

Copyright 2012 by ABC-CLIO, LLC

All rights reserved. No part of this publication may be reproduced, stored in a retrieval system, or transmitted, in any form or by any means, electronic, mechanical, photocopying, recording, or otherwise, except for the inclusion of brief quotations in a review, without prior permission in writing from the publisher.

Library of Congress Cataloging-in-Publication Data

Melton, Brian C., 1976–
Robert E. Lee: a biography / Brian C. Melton.
p. cm. — (Greenwood biographies)
Includes bibliographical references and index.
ISBN 978-0-313-38436-3 (hardcopy : alk. paper) — ISBN 978-0-313-38437-0 (ebook) 1. Lee, Robert E. (Robert Edward), 1807–1870. 2. Generals—United States—Biography. 3. Generals—Confederate States of America—Biography. 4. Confederate States of America. Army—Biography. 5. United States—History—Civil War, 1861–1865—Campaigns. I. Title.
E467.1.L4M497 2012
973.7'3092—dc23
[B] 2011050443

ISBN: 978-0-313-38436-3
EISBN: 978-0-313-38437-0

16 15 14 13 12 1 2 3 4 5

This book is also available on the World Wide Web as an eBook.
Visit www.abc-clio.com for details.

Greenwood
An Imprint of ABC-CLIO, LLC

ABC-CLIO, LLC
130 Cremona Drive, P.O. Box 1911
Santa Barbara, California 93116-1911

This book is printed on acid-free paper ∞

Manufactured in the United States of America

Copyright Acknowledgment

The poem "Appomattox" appears by permission from *Stars Through the Clouds: The Collected Poetry of Donald T. Williams* (Lynchburg: Lantern Hollow Press, 2011).

To Annora, beloved daughter.
Soli Deo Gloria.

CONTENTS

SERIES FOREWORD

In response to school and library needs, ABC-CLIO publishes this distinguished series of full-length biographies specifically for student use. Prepared by field experts and professionals, these engaging biographies are tailored for students who need challenging yet accessible biographies. Ideal for school assignments and student research, the length, format, and subject areas are designed to meet educators' requirements and students' interests.

ABC-CLIO offers an extensive selection of biographies spanning all curriculum-related subject areas including social studies, the sciences, literature and the arts, history and politics, and popular culture, covering public figures and famous personalities from all time periods and backgrounds, both historic and contemporary, who have made an impact on American and/or world culture. The subjects of these biographies were chosen based on comprehensive feedback from librarians and educators. Consideration was given to both curriculum relevance and inherent interest. Readers will find a wide array of subject choices from fascinating entertainers like Miley Cyrus and Lady Gaga to inspiring leaders like John F. Kennedy and Nelson Mandela, from the greatest athletes of our time like Michael Jordan and Lance Armstrong to the most amazing success stories of our day like J.K. Rowling and Oprah.

While the emphasis is on fact, not glorification, the books are meant to be fun to read. Each volume provides in-depth information about the subject's life from birth through childhood, the teen years, and adulthood. A thorough account relates family background and education, traces personal and professional influences, and explores struggles, accomplishments, and contributions. A timeline highlights the most significant life events against an historical perspective. Bibliographies supplement the reference value of each volume.

INTRODUCTION

WHO WAS ROBERT E. LEE?

The question "Who was Robert E. Lee?" would seem simple to answer. After all, virtually everyone knows he was a famous Confederate general. Better, even if someone by chance had never heard of him, generations of scholars have written a veritable legion of books about Lee and the events of his life, all purporting to answer that precise question. Historians have provided (combined) hundreds of years of detailed research in every minute aspect of the man's life. Some of them have devoted their entire careers to understanding his. There are people in America today who make their living just pretending to be Lee, and perhaps one of them could answer. Surely, somewhere in that mountain of information, the answers must lie.

They are there, of course, but that does not stop people from making things complicated. Lee's status as a national symbol makes his nature a very potent, emotional subject. There are many different views on who Lee was for the simple reason that there are so many different people who desperately *want* him to be so many different things. For some people, he is the invincible Southern warrior, a man who epitomized the very essence of *antebellum* culture. For others, he is a slaveholding monstrosity, a virulent racist who betrayed his country and his conscience by supporting the Confederacy and fighting for it so effectively. For still others, he is the Christian gentleman, a man who lived as perfect a moral life as is humanly possible. For each of them, the question of who Lee was is answered first, and then the evidence is sought to fit that predetermined mold.

With so many people laying claim to Lee's legacy, it is no surprise that they are willing to spend the time combing through the evidence to find points that support their own ideas. The fact that there is so much information available on Lee makes it possible to find something about him somewhere that will fit whatever view of the man people want to see. As of this writing, Amazon.com has 3,515 total items listed for Robert E. Lee, and 2,032 of these are books. If someone started reading/viewing them at a rate of one per day, that's enough material to keep them occupied for more than 6 years (11, if they work with all items). In the midst of all of that information, it is possible to find all sorts of Lees.

The good news is that "the truth is out there," and it is not hard to find if one takes the time to look. The best place to begin a study of Lee is the one point on which all scholars agree: he was human—a very unique person, true, but human nonetheless. Lee did good things, bad things, and things that were in between. Remembering this before all else keeps the reader grounded and focused. In looking at Lee as a real person (not a demigod, myth, statue, perfection incarnate, etc.), it is possible to see the man underneath. It is possible to see Lee for who he really was and not who generations of historians, movements, and (in some cases) worshippers have made him out to be.

Appomattox

"I'd rather die a thousand deaths," he'd said;
Well, better he should die them than his men.
Though there was nothing left for them to win,
Still at his word they would have fought and bled
(Or starved, more likely—true—but dead is dead).

So Lee, immaculate in his dress grays,
And Grant, unbuttoned, chewing his cigar,
Sat down together there to end the war.
And when they had agreed on every phrase,
They signed it through an inexplicable haze.

And Lee stepped out upon the porch that day
And drove his fist into his open hand
Three times while staring out across the land.
And then, since there was nothing more to say,
He mounted Traveler and rode away.

And now he'd have to face the thin gray lines.
"It's Gen'ral Lee!" With joy they gathered 'round.
He tried to speak, but could not force a sound,
'Til slowly in his face they read the signs
And silence fell beneath the somber pines.

Only those nearby could comprehend
The words, "Superior numbers . . . forced to yield . . .
Your horses you may keep to plow your fields . . .
I've done the best I could for you, my friends.
You're heroes all. Farewell." And so it ends:

The last gasp of the South that might have been,
The first breath of the South as she would be,
Beaten, bowed—but with a memory:
The independence that she could not win,
The Lost Cause, and the frailty of men.

The noblest soldier living could not save
Her from the long defeat or from the tears.
It would protect her for a hundred years
From half the vulgar lies with which men pave
The primrose paths that lead but to the grave.

For Lee stepped out upon the porch that day
And drove his fist into his open hand
Three times while staring out across the land.
And then, since there was nothing more to say,
He mounted Traveler and rode away.

—Donald T. Williams

TIMELINE: EVENTS IN THE LIFE OF ROBERT E. LEE

January 19, 1807	Robert Edward Lee born.
1811	Family moves to Alexandria, Virginia.
March 25, 1818	Henry "Light Horse" Harry Lee dies at Cumberland Island, Georgia.
1825–1829	Attends West Point. His mother dies shortly after his graduation.
1830–1855	Service with the Corps of Engineers.
June 30, 1831	Marries Mary Custis at Arlington, Virginia.
1846–1848	Serves with distinction in the Mexican War.
1852–1855	Commandant of West Point.
1855–1859	Transferred from the staff to the line, serves in Texas.
October 10, 1857	George Washington Parke Custis dies at Arlington. Lee takes an extended leave of absence to settle his estate.
October 16–18, 1859	Lee puts down John Brown's attempt to start a slave insurrection at Harpers Ferry, Virginia.
1860	Lee returns to duty with his unit in Texas.

April 16–20, 1861	Lee is offered command of U.S. Army, but resigns instead.
April 23	Lee given command of Virginia forces.
May–July	Serves as adviser to President Jefferson Davis.
June 14	Receives promotion to full general in the Confederate Army.
August–October	Fails to push the Federals out of western Virginia, is attacked in the press.
November 1861–March 1862	Davis places Lee in charge of defending Georgia and South Carolina, then recalls him to serve as adviser.
June 1, 1862	Lee is placed in command of what comes to be known as the Army of Northern Virginia after Joseph E. Johnston is wounded at Seven Pines/Fair Oaks.
June 26–July 2	The Seven Days Battles; drives George McClellan away from Richmond.
August 28–30	Lee wins the Second Battle of Bull Run/Manassas.
September 5	Lee invades Maryland.
September 17	Draws the Battle of Antietam; is forced to abandon the campaign.
December 11–15	Repels Ambrose Burnside at the Battle of Fredericksburg.
April 30–May 6, 1863	Defeats Joseph Hooker in the Battle of Chancellorsville. Thomas Jonathan "Stonewall" Jackson killed.
June	Invades Maryland and Pennsylvania.
June 30–July 3	Suffers defeat at the Battle of Gettysburg.
July 4–July 13	Successfully retreats back into Virginia.
October–December	Conducts Mine Run Campaign to no effect.
May–June 1864	Fights the defensive Overland Campaign against Ulysses S. Grant.
May 5–6	Battle of the Wilderness.
May 8–21	Fighting around Spotsylvania Courthouse.
May 31–June 12	Fighting around Cold Harbor.
June 16	Dispatches Early on what eventually becomes his raid on Washington and the Shenandoah.

June 18	Reaches Petersburg in time to prevent its fall. The Siege of Petersburg begins.
July 30	Battle of the Crater.
January 1865	Lee is appointed commander in chief of all Confederate forces.
April 2	Lee's lines break and his retreat begins. Richmond falls the next day.
April 9	Lee surrenders to Grant at Appomattox Courthouse.
August	Accepts position as president of Washington College (later Washington and Lee).
1868	Lee is forced to deal with the "Johnston Affair" at Washington College.
1868–1869	Lee's health continues to decline notably.
March–July 1870	Lee embarks on several tours to see family and medical specialists in the hopes of recovering his health.
September 27	Lee suffers a stroke that leaves him unable to speak or expectorate.
October 9	Lee dies.

Chapter 1

EARLY LIFE, EDUCATION, AND THE ENGINEERS

The small house on Cameron Street in Alexandria, Virginia, the latest home of the famous Lee family, awaited the arrival of former general and governor Henry Lee III in the late summer of 1812. Lee's wife and children no doubt looked for him with anticipation and fear. They simply did not know what to expect. Henry had been savagely beaten earlier in the summer while defending a friend's right to print federalist literature in a now rabidly democratic-republican nation gripped by a wave of wartime patriotism. After he had lost consciousness, candle wax had been poured into his eyes, he had been slashed with pen knives, and someone had removed part of his nose as a souvenir. His injuries had been so extensive that word had at first been sent that he had been killed. Instead, thanks to his powerful body, he had survived, though barely. To his family, the broken, tired man who walked through the door that day was but a shadow of his former glory. Though Harry Lee returned to his family that day with the best of intentions (he always had the best of intentions), in reality he would soon leave them again.

While the Lee family seemed at one time destined for the brightest of futures, much pain and misfortune had befallen it, and quite a bit of that was the direct responsibility of its patriarch. "Light Horse Harry"

Henry "Light Horse Harry" Lee. (Library of Congress.)

Lee had served valiantly in the American Revolution, earning a respectable share of fame and glory. While he could have remained in the army and done well, he suddenly resigned his commission in 1782 for reasons still unknown, while the war was still technically under way. Rather than rest on his laurels, he used them as a springboard to become governor of Virginia. People speculated that he might even follow his idol, George Washington, into the presidency of the United States. After the death of his first wife, he wooed and married Ann Carter, the accomplished daughter of one of the wealthiest families in the Old Dominion. Unfortunately, Henry Lee's rise to power and fortune had already peaked.

In one respect, "Light Horse Harry" resembled his most famous son's future antagonist, Ulysses S. Grant: He excelled in making war, but in all else he seemed mediocre at best. First, while still governor, he charged off to what he hoped would be martial glory under Washington during the Whiskey Rebellion. He was promptly voted out of office by the citizens of Virginia, who thought that their governor should pay more attention to affairs in their own state rather than making war in someone else's. He returned to find that he and his family had been evicted from the governor's mansion. Lee also embarked on a long string of speculations, particularly in land, and lost massive amounts of money on almost all of them. He began selling off parcels of family property to finance each big venture, always expecting the next to pay for all and watching all fail miserably. When he ran out of his own money, he started trying to drain his wife's inheritance.

Unlike Grant, however, Harry Lee tended to try to talk his way out of his debts, calling in favors and paying off only what he must to keep creditors just far enough away for his next ill-fated scheme to fail to come to fruition. His first wife's estate at Stratford Hall dwindled yearly as he sold off more and more of it to try to pay for his monetary indiscretions. When he had sold off almost all he could, the furniture went next, and eventually Stratford Hall itself passed out of Harry's hands into those of Henry Lee IV, a son from his first marriage who would live a colorful life of his own. Harry spent very little time with his second family and instead moved about quite a bit, trying in vain to resurrect his fortunes. He wrote an account of his services in the South during the war, but it failed to sell. Attempts to resurrect his military career never brought him even a tenth of the glory he had earned during his revolutionary days. Perhaps his best chance at reviving that career came when he put his name forward for commander of the American army, but, unfortunately for him, his more recent reputation preceded him. Washington himself turned Lee down, noting that though "Light Horse Harry" had military ability, he simply could not manage money.

Ann Carter Lee, his second wife, somehow managed to hold the rest of the family together in the midst of her husband's self-created maelstrom. Her father, an astute judge of character and not enthusiastic about trusting his daughter to the wild and daring governor to begin with, had provided her with independent income that Henry Lee could not access, and this gave her a measure of independence. A powerfully Christian woman, though often in weak health, Ann used her own money as wisely as her husband did foolishly and thereby provided a comfortable if spare living for their children, more of whom arrived regularly.

Robert Edward Lee arrived in this world on January 19, 1807, as the son of a bona fide American hero and a woman called by some "one of the finest women the state of Virginia ever produced." He thankfully would have far fewer memories of his father's failures than he would of his mother's successes. He was only five and a half when what was left of Harry Lee returned to the house in Alexandria. He was only six years old when his father boarded a ship for the Caribbean, never to return to his family again. For Robert, his father would remain the towering hero of the Revolution, and Robert would spend the rest of his life promoting that image. A few years before his own death in 1870, he was still defending his father's memory, and considered writing a new biography. Harry Lee's dissipation did seem to exert a significant influence on his son, particularly in the way Robert conducted his own affairs. For virtually his entire life, Robert became the very picture of self-control and responsibility, characteristics to which "Light Horse Harry" only aspired.

Robert took on many adult responsibilities early in life out of necessity. He and his older brothers, particularly Carter and Smith, took care of their ailing mother for most of their childhood. Ann suffered for years, probably from tuberculosis, a terrible, wasting disease of the lungs for which there was no cure. When Carter left for Harvard College and Smith departed to join the navy, Robert was left in charge of the family by default. Though only 13 years old at the time, he carried himself well: he managed the household, nursed his mother, and attended school. It was definitely far more responsibility than most children bore at that age.

The rest of Robert's formative years saw him caring devotedly for his mother, surrounded primarily by women. In fact, when his mother faced the prospect of his departure she lamented "How can I live without Robert? He is both son and daughter to me." That, in many ways, sums up quite a bit of Robert's eventual personality and social traits. He exhibited the best of both sexual stereotypes. This would lead to a number of apparent contradictions. In a matter of moments he could go from a grinding insistent use of power to viciously pursue his opponents on the battlefield to a tender, nurturing approach in interpersonal relationships. Sometimes both aspects of his personality manifested at once. In those moments, the lingering specters of both Ann and "Light Horse Harry" seemed to haunt Robert simultaneously. Another manifestation of Ann's influence (and perhaps Harry's) was demonstrated in his preferred choice of company: women. Robert always seemed to have a stronger rapport with ladies than with men and demonstrated this tendency at an early age.

Robert's early education was in the classical style at Alexandria Academy under William B. Leary. He learned quite a bit about languages, particularly Latin and Greek, in addition to mathematics and science. This allowed him to read many of the great authors of antiquity in their original languages, including Homer, Tacitus, and Cicero. His reading and early linguistic studies prepared him to more fully play the role of educated Virginia gentleman later in life. Perhaps more important, the classical model of education focuses as much attention on *how* to think as the modern approach does on *what* to think. That foundation would serve him well when, later in life, he would be forced to reason creatively in response to seemingly impossible situations.

As Lee's late teen years approached, his family members turned their attention to his eventual profession, but it was not obvious what direction he should take. It was by no means clear that he would become a military man, and, if he did, he might not join the army. His brother Smith had already gone to sea with the navy and Carter attended Harvard before settling down to practice law in New York City. Robert probably considered several alternatives to the army, but obviously found them less than inviting. Though he was a practicing Christian, he had not developed the deep and pronounced faith he would exhibit later in life. Also, he had a marked aversion to public speaking and never felt competent in front of a classroom. This likely led him away from careers in the church, in education, or in law. Another important factor in the equation was the family's relative poverty. Though they had never wanted for food or shelter, if Robert's career choice would require any further funds for schooling, Ann's budget would not be able to provide it—it would have to pay for itself. Therefore, all things considered, the Lees decided to pursue an appointment for him at the United States Military Academy at West Point. It seemed to answer all of his problems and desires nicely.

Once Robert's course had been decided, the problem then became how to set him on it. First, he began his own preparation by leaving his classical education behind and pursuing specific studies in science and mathematics with Benjamin Hallowell in Alexandria. The larger problem was admission. West Point has never simply accepted applicants, as other institutions of higher learning do. At the time, all appointments were made personally by the secretary of war (John C. Calhoun, in this case). The family therefore had to find a way to convince Calhoun to choose Robert, and their campaign began in earnest in early 1824. Robert introduced himself to Calhoun with a letter from William Fitzhugh, who owned the house in which the Lees were currently residing. The family called upon every political acquaintance on their list of allies, and eventually six letters carrying the signatures of congressmen, senators, and Robert's half brother "Black Horse Harry" made their way onto Calhoun's desk. Though the competition was keen that year, Calhoun appointed Robert, but deferred his actual starting date until July 1825.

West Point had gone through of a bit of a revolution before Lee arrived. Though Thomas Jefferson founded West Point in 1802, the quality of its education and the state of its facilities had varied widely since. At times, standards had degenerated to the point that the government had very seriously considered closing the school entirely. That changed with the appointment of Colonel Sylvanus Thayer. Thayer transformed the academy into a strong teaching institution that emphasized honor, respect, and military discipline. He focused his curriculum on engineering and mathematics. The very best of its graduates went into the corps of engineers, the second best into the artillery, and the rest into the infantry. Ironically, cadets received relatively little training in campaign strategy and battlefield tactics.

Lee's performance at West Point proved to be exemplary. In his four years there, he did not accrue a single demerit for any infraction of the rules. While Lee's feat is rare, there are other cases on record of other cadets equaling it. Academically, he ranked first in his class for three of his four years, beaten in his final year by Charles Mason of New York. Ironically, Mason did not distinguish himself as a military man later in life. He taught classes at West Point for one year before resigning and moving west, where he became a solid citizen of Burlington, Iowa.

West Point left its mark on Cadet Lee in a number of ways that would impact his future apart from his particular studies. While there, Lee first encountered the military culture that would mark the rest of his life. He thrived under the harsh discipline and ordered existence of the Thayer era. Its austere, ordered way of life became a part of the fiber of

Lee's being and he exhibited his preference for it from West Point all the way to his sparse study at what would become Washington and Lee University. The people he met and the friendships he formed also became another important legacy of Lee's time at West Point. His future commander in chief, Jefferson Davis, graduated only one year ahead of Lee, and fellow Virginian Joseph E. Johnson, an eventual competitor for command of the Army of Northern Virginia, became one of Lee's closest friends.

When Lee left West Point in 1829, the army appointed him a brevet (honorary) second lieutenant and he entered the Corps of Engineers. He had developed in physical stature as well as intellectual ability during the previous four years. Lee stood at 5 feet, 11 inches—quite tall in a time when the average man only reached about 5 feet, 4 inches. While his strict military bearing distinguished him, it also left him a little stiff. Most people (especially the ladies) agreed that Lee was one of the most handsome men in the South. His dark eyes, broad, muscular frame, impeccable manners, and gentlemanly bearing won him many admirers. He had also redeemed the Lee name from its former reputation for burning through money; unlike almost all the other Southern cadets, Lee left West Point with a significantly positive balance due him from the business office.

Upon graduation, all the cadets received two months leave. Lee returned as quickly as he could to his mother's home in Virginia. Ann was finally succumbing to the tuberculosis with which she had struggled for decades. Though she had seemed to rally for a short time earlier in the spring, by the time Lee arrived at her bedside she was very near death. There was little he could do aside from make her as comfortable as he could, be as positive as honesty would allow, and wait for the end. Ann Hill Carter Lee passed away in July 1829. She left remarkably little behind her for future generations to use to understand her. There are very few letters known to be hers, a dress that could have belonged to her, and a portrait allegedly of her. Her most important and telling legacy was her youngest son.

While Lee would lose one important woman in his life in 1829, he took steps toward gaining another. Over the course of the summer, Lee visited with family and friends he had not seen since a trip home from West Point two years before. Mary Randolph Custis was one of many friends with whom he reacquainted himself. She was a friend of a friend of Lee's sister Mildred, and they both had ties to other families that meant they saw a good deal of each other that summer. Overall, Mary was an attractive girl, though somewhat plain. She was well read and intelligent, and in her subsequent letters often gave the flirtatious Lee as hard a time as he gave her. She was notable more for her lineage than for any personal accomplishment of her own: She was the great granddaughter of Martha Washington, and, by adoption, the granddaughter of George. Her father, George Washington Parke Custis, had lived his entire life as the "Boy of Mt. Vernon," enjoying a significant inheritance from Martha, and he passed along his distinguished status to his beloved and pampered daughter. While it is impossible to tell exactly how quickly the romantic relationship developed, by the time Lee left Virginia for his first official post, he had secured permission to write to Mary.

In August, the War Department ordered Lee to Savannah, Georgia, to a place called Cockspur Island. Only a mile long, it was made up of thick, sticky marsh mud that never dried completely. Most of the island flooded when the tide came in and any large storms swamped it completely. It did have one redeeming characteristic, however: It dominated the mouth of the strategically important Savannah River, which flows along the border between Georgia and South Carolina. Lee was supposed to assist in preparing the island to handle the load of the massive fortifications that the army planned to build there. That would involve the construction of ditches and dikes to drain the land and allow it to be successfully reinforced. The work would be seasonal, since conditions in the summer prevented much, if any, progress from being made. When Lee arrived with a slave named Nat as his servant, he found that his superior officer, Major Samuel Babcock, had decided to direct the work from afar, leaving the young Lee to take up the considerable slack Babcock's absence created. With Babcock gone, Lee was in de facto charge of the project, something he resented.

When Lee got the occasional chance to escape to Savannah, he found a relaxing, pleasurable, and genteel atmosphere that doubtlessly made Cockspur Island seem a continent away. One of Lee's friends from West Point, Jack Mackay, was not only from Savannah but had been posted to an artillery company there and Lee often visited him and his family. Mackay's mother quickly adopted Lee, even assigning him his own room. Though Lee could only make it to Savannah about once every two weeks, his connection to the Mackays ensured that his time there was more than simply pleasant. Mrs. Mackay also had four daughters in addition to her son, and Lee flirted with them constantly. Lee seems to have considered Margaret Mackay as a marriage prospect in addition to Mary Custis, though nothing ever came of it.

Work progressed steadily and when Babcock officially suspended efforts for the summer, Lee returned to Virginia. While there, he spent as much time in the company of Mary as he could. Before long, the dashing young engineer and his very historically grounded young lady decided to get married. While Mrs. Custis approved, Mr. Custis did not, and therefore by the time Lee returned to Cockspur Island the proposed marriage was still technically unsettled. Custis, a very stereotypical doting father, was no doubt concerned about losing his daughter and he probably had doubts about Lee's ability to support Mary (and any grandchildren that might come from their union) on the painfully small salary the army paid him. In reality, though, everyone's minds were made up but Mr. Custis's, and, whether he knew it or not, he would have little practical say in the matter. As Lee himself remarked in a letter to his older brother, "I am engaged to Miss Mary C. . . . That is, she & her mother have given their consent. But the father has not yet made up his mind, though it is supposed he will not object." Lee and the women began laying the groundwork for a wedding in the spring of 1831, realistically confident that Custis would indulge his daughter in this, as he had in all else.

The intervening winter was a pleasant one for Lee personally, as he availed himself of the company of the Mackays, but professionally it was frustrating. Lee returned to Cockspur Island to discover that summer and autumn gales had destroyed almost all of their work from the previous year, which had to then be started over again. Babcock never did return to duty that year; he was arrested, resigned from the army, and replaced by Lieutenant Joseph K. F. Mansfield, an officer later killed facing Lee's army at Antietam. Mansfield completely redesigned the project, which would come to be known as Ft. Pulaski. Whether by design or luck, Lee would not be there to see the fort the Federals would later break down go up. Not long after Mansfield's arrival, he received orders to move to Old Pointe, Virginia, near Ft. Monroe. This of course brought him back to his beloved state and much nearer Arlington Plantation, the home of his future bride.

While Lee returned to Virginia that April, he did not arrive at Arlington until the actual day of his wedding, wishing, like many men, to avoid as much of the bustle and frustration of preparation as possible. When *the* day at last arrived on June 30, 1831, Lee said he felt "as bold as a sheep," though for some reason he could not bring himself to be significantly nervous, and he vaguely reproved himself for being so calm. Lee and Mary remained at Arlington for about a week before taking a brief tour of Washington and various plantations as a honeymoon.

Lee and Mary could hardly have been two more contrasting personalities. Lee was the hardworking, disciplined son of a poor, respectable mother and a father whose memory he strove to vindicate. He had worked hard for what he had earned and was careful to shepherd his resources. The young soldier's mind was organized, his life ordered, and his word his bond. Mary, on the other hand, was the pampered daughter of a rich father who indulged her every whim. Though her inherent good character and the nurture of her mother had prevented such an upbringing from ruining her entirely, she took a distinct view of life when compared to her husband and his expectations. To Robert, any appointment was to be taken seriously and kept with strict punctuality. For Mary, appointments were general guidelines she kept when she could. Robert expected the home kept clean and neat, and he felt it was his wife's duty to make sure it stayed that way. Mary agreed that housework should be seen to in great detail—by the servants. There were better ways to spend her time. Differences of opinion such as these led to the inevitable stress that any marriage must weather in order to succeed.

Another possible source of frustration for Mary might have been Robert's continuing lively letter writing with his female acquaintances. Throughout his life, but particularly in his younger days, Lee kept up an amazingly frank correspondence with a number of ladies. Though draped in thinly veiled metaphor, these letters virtually exuded Lee's potent sexuality. For instance, he wrote to one of the Mackay sisters, asking if, on her wedding night, did she "go off well, like a torpedo cracker on Christmas morning?" While it is possible that the apparent reference to the pleasure of her wedding night was simply incidental, it is not likely given the universal nature of man. After all, at that point, he and Mary

A portrait of Mary Lee, painted seven years after her marriage to Robert. (Library of Congress.)

clearly had firsthand knowledge of the subject, so much so that just after their marriage, Lee complained to his brother, "I actually could not find *time* before I left [Arlington after the ceremony] for anything except—." Over time, Lee grew more circumspect in his choice of language, but his flirtatious side never disappeared completely. Even in his old age, he could be found teasing pretty girls when opportunity and decorum permitted.

Lee's descriptive admiration of women other than Mary emerged most often when he was alone and separated from her and his family. He was a passionate man and, when he felt lonely, his mind tended to wander. With his ability to connect with women so easily, his correspondence was littered with suggestions and implications that could belong equally well in the mouth of a frank friend or a paramour. Lee wrote of the "Daughters of Eve . . . [who] would make your lips water and your fingers tingle," and described another young woman as sitting "during dinner expanding her large eyes & pouting her pretty lips & has all the appearance of one that has not found matrimony what it is cracked up to be." One lady even "admitted me [Lee] (an innocent man) into her bed chamber a few days after" a dance.

Despite recent rumors, there is no historical evidence to suggest that Lee ever crossed the line from inappropriate thinking into inappropriate conduct, especially after his marriage to Mary. In fact, one of the distinguishing characteristics of his relationships of this sort was how he tried to include Mary in them by making her a part of the correspondence when he could, even giving the letter containing the "torpedo cracker" comment above for her to append her signature (and doubtless read). Perhaps this was his way of legitimatizing the associations; perhaps it was his way of building safeguards against taking them too far. There certainly is no sense in his letters that he was attempting to hide them from Mary and he obviously did not destroy them. While it is impossible to prove a negative, at the very least it seems quite unlikely that Lee actually engaged in any illicit affairs, however attracted he may have been to his various female friends. His correspondence may seem somewhat suspect to a modern audience, but Lee was not a modern man and he did not live in the modern world.

Of course, this side of Lee sounds strange to readers who know Lee better as a form of Confederate deity than as an actual human being. Lee himself probably looked back at his earlier letters and flirtations with some regret and considerable embarrassment. In reality, Lee's passionate and, at times, bawdy letters reveal a very human heart inside a marble man subject to very human desires and temptations. Only the mistaken tendency to treat Lee as a figure of Christ-like perfection (see the latter half of chapter eight) can interpret this as "cheapening" Lee's memory. Contrarily, it sets a powerful example: If Lee could control such potent impulses and even turn them to his advantage as a good, moral man, then it is possible for others to do so as well.

Lee's time at Ft. Monroe was professionally productive but also frustrating. He spent his time building up the foundation of a fort, much like he had in Georgia. Here, though, the engineering problem was much simpler and Lee spent most of his time overseeing workers pouring sand and stone into the water to form a stable, artificial island. The frustration came from the sheer drudgery of the work and a running "war" between the artillery and the engineers, both of whom struggled for control of the project. Of more importance, he demonstrated to his superiors that he was an able, efficient officer who could be trusted to handle significant projects independently.

On a personal level, Lee found Ft. Monroe pleasant, and he and Mary seemed to settle into their new lives with a minimum of controversy and strain. They initially shared quarters with another family, the Talcotts, who became close friends, but they later moved into several rooms of their own. Mary seems to have adjusted to her newer, poorer existence quite well, helped, no doubt by the relief from work brought by several slaves she had taken with her from Arlington. Robert expressed frustration with her at times, but the two of them genuinely loved each other, and he seemed to adopt a patient, supportive attitude toward her, as he had his mother. The similarities between the Mrs. Lees became more evident when Mary fell ill. Robert cared for her devotedly and she recovered, but this foreshadowed a pattern they would follow for the rest of their lives.

Lee spent only a few years at Old Pointe. His commanders in Washington offered him a chance to escape the petty bickering between engineers and artillery—which the artillery eventually won. General Charles Gratiot, in charge of the Corps of Engineers, asked Lee to come to Washington to serve as his assistant. In November 1834, Lee officially moved to Washington, usually commuting across the Potomac to work each morning from his father-in-law's home at Arlington, sometimes staying in a boarding house with his old friend Joe Johnston.

Washington was a useful post for Lee, if somewhat boring. Gratiot often absented himself and trusted Lee with the day-to-day running of the office, though, unlike Babcock, Gratiot was kept away by the legitimate business of far-flung inspections. Aside from one significant side trip to help survey the border between Michigan and Ohio in 1835, Lee spent his time compiling reports, organizing paperwork, and lobbying Congress. He found the system of patronage, in which officers must secure some sort of political backing for promotion, to be annoying and unfair, but he learned to function within it. His position brought him into contact with quite a few significant officers and politicians on the national level. Mary, when she was not ill, enjoyed this time as much as any other in her life. She loved being at home with her parents and having her own family there too. By the time they left, she had added two children to the mix, Custis and Mary. Her health took a significant turn for the worse after Mary's birth, and she never really recovered. Even so, she would eventually bear Robert a total of seven children.

The combination of Mary's health woes and his apparent professional stagnation frustrated Lee, though Gratiot did what he could to assuage his young assistant. He managed to get Lee a promotion to first lieutenant, but Lee was still restless. He preferred, he said to his brother Carter, to be out of the office and in the field, "diversifying the scene, amusing the mind, and endeavoring to strengthen the body." While Lee was referring to a vacation, it applied to his larger life as well. This would lead to tension with Mary, since as a result of her husband's wanderlust, she would rarely see him. Though he made a point of taking his family with him when the situation permitted, Mary's health and the children made that difficult and sometimes the conditions of his post made it impossible. During their married life, he spent as much time away from her as he did with her.

Gratiot soon sent Lee on his next engineering adventure. The burgeoning city of St. Louis, Missouri, was a port on the Mississippi River and it had a problem. The "Father of Waters" has always been a fickle friend to its neighbors. Though it may be hard to believe a river a mile wide can change its course with little apparent warning, it somehow manages to do so. St. Louis's prime source of income was its access to the Mississippi, and the river was showing signs that it planned to move elsewhere. A large sandbar called Duncan's Island was growing rapidly as the river deposited tons of sand and sediment against it. As it did so, the island slowly closed off access to the port. In addition to addressing this issue, Lee had also been assigned to clear two sets of difficult rapids in order to improve navigation.

Lee was, like his father, a good federalist, even though that political party no longer technically existed, and this was precisely the type of job that fell in line with his political beliefs. With the federalists, he believed in a strong national government and leadership by societal elites. This sort of public works project, where the government used its resources to improve and expand the country in the West would have fit well with that outlook. He took a dark view of pure democracy, seeing it as dangerous to give power to people in no position to know what was best, right, and good for the country just because they had an uninformed opinion to share. This led him to associate himself more with the Whig Party of Henry Clay, which promised to keep the Jacksonian mobs in check and promote national interests.

Lee's time in Missouri proved to be one of the most intellectually stimulating periods of his engineering career. While the rapids were easily dealt with from a technical standpoint—they involved mostly blasting rock from the channels—the St. Louis question was more difficult. Lee's solution demonstrated intelligence, flexibility, and creativity. Rather than fight the river, he proposed a series of dikes and barriers to channel the full force of the Mississippi away from the Illinois shore and directly toward Duncan's Island. In theory, the river would wash the island away and deepen the port at the same time.

The plans for St. Louis were indeed good, and they likely would have worked even better if Lee had been able to implement all of them. Unfortunately, his political education continued as various interests and factions got in his way. A citizen across the river from St. Louis in Brooklyn, Illinois filed a court injunction in order to have the work stopped. Brooklyn would have been the undoubted beneficiary from a change in the river's course, and stood to become a new port in the area if things were allowed to proceed, and that led to all sorts of investment potential. Lee, who had only just started to make serious progress, had to suspend work until the matter was cleared up. He then had to face problems obtaining workers and equipment. Even when he was able to get his materials together, Congress had a nasty habit of selling him short in terms of funding.

Lee's departure from the project was anti-climactic. He came home to Arlington at the end of 1839, unsure of where he would go next. It made sense for him to return to Missouri, but Congress refused to fund the project further. Lee's new superior, Colonel Joseph G. Totten, ordered Lee to make one last trip to account for and then sell off the government equipment. Over all, Lee had been able to implement enough of his plans to make a significant difference in the area. He was able to improve the passage through the rapids notably. While his plan for St. Louis was only partially completed, his dikes redirected enough of the Mississippi's flow to wash Duncan's Island away, thereby saving St. Louis harbor. Thanks to Lee's contributions, the city continued its rise in the commercial world.

By this point, Lee had achieved enough fame and seniority in the Corps to warrant some input on his next choice of assignment. He was given several options, including another posting to Washington, one to New York City, and a position at West Point as an instructor. Lee turned West Point down quickly, saying that he believed there was "an *art* in imparting . . . knowledge, and in making a subject agreeable to those that learn that I have never found that I possessed. . . ." Perhaps worse in Lee's mind, gaining faculty positions at West Point had become a very political affair and if Lee made a mistake, he could damage his career prospects. He also wanted to avoid another pure assistantship in Washington, a job that would amount to becoming an office manager. Instead, he chose to go to New York.

The engineering aspects of the New York assignment were decidedly less than exciting. Lee would be in charge of refurbishing several forts in Brooklyn. The forts did not need significant re-engineering, and Lee faced mundane problems such as replacing rotten wood in gun emplacements and repairing water leaks in the various ramparts. Handling these problems would not be difficult, but Lee's thorough professionalism ensured the job was well done. He did not fully escape status as an assistant, and worked with Totten in that capacity in 1844. He also served on the Board of Visitors for West Point in 1844 and on the Board of Engineers for the Atlantic Coastal Defense from 1845 to 1848. He repaired, designed, evaluated, sketched, and filled out paperwork, but did not accomplish anything on the scale of the work he had undertaken at St. Louis.

Professionally, Lee's life from 1840 until 1846 did not seem to amount to much, but personally he was very much embroiled in the reality of fatherhood. Mary and the children came to live with him in rooms in New York. Robert had already been concerned about Mary's ability as a mother, and he had tried to engage in parenting by letter. He admonished Mary to take a firmer hand with Fitzhugh (Rooney, as he was known to most), who Lee said had acquired "the reputation of being hard to manage." He had gone a step farther, writing Mary's mother and asking that she take a hand and force Mary to make good decisions when it came to the children. He read several books on parenting and tried to put them into practice as best he could from afar. Now that his family would be back with him, he would be able to do so in person.

For her part, Mary no doubt tried her best, but her own training for motherhood left her in a difficult place, especially given Robert's high standards. She tried to raise her children as she herself had been raised, with far more indulgence than discipline. Mary had come up in the stereotypical Southern plantation household, and so most of the uncomfortable work, from mothering to cooking to cleaning, had been done by the family's slaves. After her marriage to Robert, she had no particular desire to change, even though her husband regularly gave her a litany of reasons to do so. Robert's regular absence and continued attempts to enforce discipline by proxy probably increased her feelings of guilt more than it helped her. Finally, Mary's body had always been weak and the regular ordeals of childbirth and illnesses left her broken down for months at a time, making her pursuit of Robert's ideal of motherhood all the more difficult.

Lee's approach to fatherhood in the years when he was around his family emphasized both self-control and attentive care. Overall, he adopted many of the maxims his contemporaries impressed upon him through the books he had read. He took every opportunity to turn every misstep into a teaching moment. One misadventure that befell Rooney provides the classic example used by most historians. Rooney, bored one day while his parents were both gone, wandered into the barn, a place that had been declared off limits to him. While exploring the hayloft, the boy somehow managed to slice off the ends of two of his fingers, one all the way at the first joint. One of the family's slaves retrieved the severed bits and rushed Rooney to the doctor, who was absent in New York at the time. When he returned, the doctor tried to reattach the finger ends, telling the family that there was a chance they would take.

Lee used the incident to instruct his other children on several occasions. He first wrote of it in a letter to Custis, who was away at school in Virginia. He told Custis of the disaster, pointing out that Rooney had specifically disobeyed by leaving the yard without permission and noting that "you see the fruits of disobedience." "He may probably lose his fingers & be ruined for life. . . . Do take warning from the calamity that has befallen your brother." Lee added, "I am now watching by his bedside lest he should disturb his hand in his sleep. I still hope his hand may be restored." He went farther a few weeks later, once it was clear that Rooney's fingers would not heal properly. He had Rooney dictate a letter to Custis, announcing that he had lost the tips. Lee took his son's dictation and had him emphasize the plea that "neither of us will disobey our parents."

Given that many modern families have adopted the much more permissive parenting models pioneered in the 1950s and 1960s, such gory detail and morbid injunctions may seem excessive. On the contrary, they reveal in Lee a strong desire to be the best parent he could be and a clear, compassionate love for his family. Given that this was the most popular parenting model of the time, Lee was applying the results of his study as best he could. It is, after all, hard to hold to a softer standard that did not exist at the time. More important, Lee cared for his sons' futures far more than he valued their immediate contentment. He was willing to push them past where they were comfortable in order to ensure that they would make better choices in the future. As any parent will admit, punishing children in any way is more difficult that indulging them.

Still, if enforcing discipline through various punishments represented the totality of Lee's personality as a parent, he would have been a poor one indeed. But Lee coupled his iron discipline with tender care. As noted above, Lee did not simply rail against Rooney's indiscretion or use it as leverage in the hope of guilting Custis into better behavior; he quite literally stood by Rooney through his long nights of pain and regret. In lighter times, he also spent quality time playing with his children. Often, at the end of a long day, Lee would enlist his children in tickling his feet, something he enjoyed immensely. He would tell them stories as they all relaxed, and if they began to nod off, he would tickle them with his feet to wake them up, laughing along with them. If that failed, he simply reminded them, "No tickling, no story!"

As Lee worked on his string of smaller jobs and raised his family, tensions between the United States and Mexico had been growing. As far back as the war for its independence, the Republic of Texas had wanted to be annexed to the United States. The United States, however, had not acted, because Mexico had continued to claim ownership of the land, and to annex Texas could lead to war. At the time, Mexico had a significantly larger army than the United States, and therefore the threat of war could not be taken lightly. President John Tyler finally decided the issue by annexing Texas in early 1845. The argument then became over what specifically he had annexed. The United States claimed significantly more land than the Mexicans were willing to cede. Tyler's successor, President James K. Polk posted troops into the disputed land to maintain the U.S. claim.

As the disagreement intensified, Lee knew what course he wanted to take. He had served 17 years in the Corps of Engineers, and had been satisfied with his role building, constructing, and maintaining. Now that war with another country loomed, Lee wanted to get into the business of breaking things. He was even willing to leave the Corps if necessary. As he wrote Totten in June of 1845, "In the event of war with any foreign government I should desire to be brought into active service in the field with as high a rank in the regular army as I could obtain." Perhaps the ghost of "Light Horse Harry" was once again rattling his chains in his son's mind, but it was clear that if war with Mexico was in the offing, Robert Lee wanted to be a prominent part of it.

Chapter 2

THE MEXICAN WAR, TEXAS, AND JOHN BROWN

Robert E. Lee, one of the best known and most respected members of the Corps of Engineers, watched the burgeoning crisis with Mexico closely. Lee was now approaching 40 years old, and though he still retained his strong sense of self-control and impressive good looks, he was also keenly aware of his encroaching age. As seen in a picture of Lee taken near this time, he had rid himself of the prominent sideburns he had sported earlier in life in favor of a large and distinguished mustache. His dark wavy hair still hung down over the top of his ears, but had not begun to take on the silver sheen that later generations would come to know so well from likenesses made during the Civil War. It was perhaps a feeling that his life was quickly passing that made Lee want to see real combat and face serious risks in the upcoming conflict.

As far as the war went, President James K. Polk tried not to disappoint Lee's hopes. Polk was an avowed expansionist, and saw in the debate with Mexico an opportunity to make significant strides toward Manifest Destiny—the idea that the United States would one day overspread the entire North American continent. Though he did nothing overtly offensive, Polk kept American troops in the disputed territory, and Santa Ana, the dictator of Mexico, obliged Polk by attacking in early 1846.

Robert E. Lee at about 40 years of age. (Library of Congress.)

Polk went to Congress seeking a declaration of war, stating that American troops had been attacked on American soil. This was, of course, a slight fabrication since the land was still disputed, but it had the desired effect. Though the Whig Party opposed the war as best it could, Polk got his declaration. Lee received orders to depart for Mexico in August 1846. Though his experiences would make him much more circumspect later in life, at the time Lee could not wait to get into the war.

Lee was ordered to join the army of Brigadier General John E. Wool, whose small force was assembling in San Antonio, Texas. After an interesting but uneventful trip, Lee arrived at Wool's camp on September 29, 1846, just before the army departed. He joined the Engineer Company, which was, in theory, responsible for building roads, bridges, and so forth. While the engineers did indeed build a few things during the campaign, they also took on a very important new role: they became pathfinders. The Mexican War was the first time the United States army had undertaken a sustained campaign in a foreign country, and it was ill prepared in some ways. There were very few detailed, reliable maps available, and the army quickly found that it relied on Mexican guides at its own peril. So the engineers began scouting in front of the army, reporting on the strengths and weaknesses of enemy positions, and leading the various parts of the army to their destinations. As a result of their new role, the engineers also began to advise the commanding generals in tactics and strategy.

During the campaign, Wool's small army fluctuated from a low of about 1,400 men to a high of about 2,000 and unfortunately accomplished nothing of note. His initial march had almost brought his men into the fight when word arrived that the Mexicans had agreed to an armistice of eight weeks after their major loss at the Battle of Monterrey. Lee vented his frustration about the delay, arguing in his letters home that "by all means advantage should have been taken of our success." Already he was demonstrating an instinctive desire to press his enemies and make the most of any situation.

Fortunately for the Mexicans, Captain Lee was not in command. The Mexican army had a chance to recover by the time the armistice came to an end and Wool could move forward. When Wool did advance, very little happened to him or to his men. Lee spent his time scouting in front of the army, sometimes leaving camp as early as 3 A.M. and riding more than 50 miles before the day had ended. While rumors abounded of massive Mexican forces, none of them proved true and for months, even while in the middle of a war, Lee managed to see little of it. His letters home mostly described the food and sights of the Mexican countryside.

Meanwhile, Polk faced a bit of a quandary. So far, General Zachary Taylor had performed very well and had won several significant victories in the north of Mexico. As a result of the various campaigns, the United States had taken control of California, New Mexico, Arizona, and several other provinces. At this point, Polk had expected to be able to negotiate an end to the war, but Santa Ana, confident of his skills as the self-proclaimed "Napoleon of the West," wanted to keep fighting. That turned a military problem into a political one for Polk.

The issue was that Polk's two highest ranking generals—Taylor and Winfield Scott—were both prominent Whigs. Polk, a Democrat, had to think about the upcoming presidential election and could not help but notice that successful generals had an annoying tendency to get elected. Since there was no Democratic general in the army, Polk needed to figure out a way to win the war without creating a Whig candidate that no one in his own party could hope to defeat. Taylor's political plans had been rapidly expanding in relation to his success on the battlefield, and Winfield Scott had already been talking about a run, even before he had won any fights. In the end, Polk decided to try to spread the victories around between Taylor and Scott. He hoped that by doing so he might mitigate the effect they would have and perhaps even set one Whig against the other. He ordered Taylor to hold his position in the north and let Scott embark on a campaign of his own.

Scott's plan, one which he had argued in favor of for quite some time, was to go straight for the proverbial throat of Mexico: Mexico City itself. Scott planned to pull another army together and assault the stronghold of Vera Cruz on the gulf coast. From there, he would march inland and approach Mexico City from the east. Ironically, his proposed route would closely mirror that of Hernando Cortez when that infamous conquistador had conquered the Aztecs centuries earlier.

So, in January 1847, Lee responded to orders sending him to join Scott's headquarters staff. He left on his 40th birthday, January 19, 1847, and along with his superior, Joseph Totten, quickly became part of what Scott called his "little cabinet." This informal advisory group served as Scott's inner circle during the upcoming campaign. By February they were under way and headed for Vera Cruz. They arrived over two weeks early for the set opening of the campaign.

While Scott's army bobbed up and down in the waters off Mexico waiting for the rest of the invasion force to arrive, Lee spent his time trapped aboard the USS *Massachusetts*. With very little to do, he passed the days writing to his family, sharing his stateroom with a seasick Joe Johnston. From these letters it is clear that Lee's burgeoning mid-life crisis continued unabated. He missed his wife and children, but he wrote them a good deal of advice, pleading with them to behave themselves and make him proud while he was away. To his mother-in-law, he lamented that up to that point in his life, "I have done no good. I hope I have escaped any great crime."

Lee performed excellently in the campaign for Mexico City. In a very real sense he became Scott's eyes, though he was by no means the only scout doing good work. Lee repeatedly identified key routes through the countryside that opened into the enemy's flank and rear, and then he himself led the forces Scott dispatched into positions where they could take advantage of his discoveries. During the battles of Contreras and Churubusco in August, as Emory Thomas summarized: "[Lee] had been awake and active for thirty-six hours (at least), crossed the Pedregal [a supposedly impassable lava field] in the dark, and led U.S. forces to crucial positions in two separate battles. . . ." After he had recovered, he then threw himself into the battles around Mexico City in September 1847. At Chapultepec, he stayed awake for another 36-hour stint until a small wound and sheer exhaustion combined to make him faint and fall out of the saddle. It was with no real exaggeration that Scott would write of the "gallant and indefatigable Captain Lee." Lee earned brevet promotions all the way to colonel for his brave conduct and hard work. This brought him to the attention of many, particularly Scott, who almost idolized his subordinate as the ideal solider. Scott would take Lee on as his informal protégé over the next 10 years.

In Scott's campaign, Lee saw war first hand, came under fire, and watched the intelligent management of an army from the general's elbow. The Mexican War gave Lee and many of his fellow officers the practical training in making war that West Point had not. Under Scott, Lee saw an army significantly inferior in numbers defeat a more powerful opponent, often by using good intelligence gathering that led to swift, decisive maneuvers. Lee already had a predisposition for aggressive warfare, and now he saw it modeled in Scott. The result became almost axiomatic for how he would manage his Civil War battles: Know more about the terrain than your opponent, seize the initiative, and drive home your advantage when victorious.

The conflict taught Lee another lesson that would serve him later on the Confederate home front: politics always precede and follow war. During the course of the fighting, Lee had tolerated the presence of Gideon Pillow, a major general of volunteers whose primary qualification was his status as one of Polk's cronies. Pillow went to war to do nothing more or less than win battles to increase his status with potential voters. It was no surprise to men like Lee, who saw duty to God, country, and his fellow men as supreme, that Pillow emerged as one of the worst generals of the war. That did not stop Pillow from grasping for more than his fair share of the laurels. Indeed, almost before the gun barrels had cooled,

Pillow and men like him scrambled to squeeze as much political capital out of their experiences as they could. For some, it meant leveraging politicians to land promotions in the army, for others, like Pillow, it meant using rank to gain more votes in the polls back at home. A particularly nasty quarrel that plainly disgusted Lee opened among Scott, Pillow, General William Worth, and Colonel James Duncan. Lee saw the bickering as completely pointless.

Lee returned to Arlington on June 29, 1848, after an absence of two years. When he rode up to the house, at first only the family dog recognized him. "Spec" ran out into the yard barking happily. The rest of the family soon joined him and the joyful reunion moved into the entrance hall. Little Rob, now four and a half years old, had prepared for his father's homecoming by dressing up in his best. He waited nervously in the background with a friend, Armistead Lippitt. When Robert the Elder looked around, suddenly asked, "Where is my little boy?" and strode over toward his son, Robert the Younger happily waited for his hug. To the lasting embarrassment of both, the father missed his son and scooped up a very surprised Lippitt instead. Clearly, Lee had some reconnecting to do with his family. Lee got the chance for some well-deserved rest when Totten assigned him to his Washington office and had him finish a number of maps he had begun while in Mexico.

After a few months of relative relaxation at Arlington and Washington, it seemed that Lee would be headed back to the same sort of work that he had done so well before the war broke out. Ft. McHenry in Baltimore Harbor had done excellent service in the War of 1812, even inspiring what later became the national anthem with its stubborn resistance, but military technology had advanced to the point that it was no longer practical. Baltimore needed to be defended from farther away and the engineers had singled out Soller's Point as the place to do it, farther downstream from the city. It would be Lee's job—between trips up and down the East Coast visiting various projects—to get the site ready to support the massive weight of what became Ft. Carroll. Starting in 1849, Lee spent the next three years engaged in providing the fort with a solid foundation. While that may have been somewhat anti-climactic after the excitement of his Mexican War performance, it gave him another opportunity to be with his family. During this time, he managed to secure a spot for his eldest son, Custis, at West Point.

If Lee was getting restless at Soller's Point, he still preferred it to the orders he received in May 1852. The War Department directed him to take over the position of superintendent at West Point. Lee had previously turned down an appointment there; it was still haunted by Sylvanus Thayer's metaphorical ghost. Any misstep could conceivably snowball into a situation that could do serious harm to the future of his career, and the system was so locked up in Thayerian traditionalism that there would be little to no opportunity to bring about substantive improvement. Given those points and Lee's unshakable belief that he was a hopeless teacher, he felt that he had nothing to give the school and yet would risk quite a bit for no real reward. He appealed the decision through his connections, but got no response, and so, in August of 1852, Lee returned to West Point, his family following afterward.

Lee found the physical campus much changed from his time as a cadet. All of the buildings he had known were gone, replaced and supplemented with more modern structures. Of course, Lee had visited West Point several times during his career when he served on the Board of Examiners, so the differences were not as stark as they otherwise would have been. The beautiful surroundings of the New York countryside had remained the same. The basic educational philosophy and attitudes of the administration had also changed very little. A supporting board of Thayer worshipers made sure that they replaced themselves with others of their ilk, and everyone took care to do things Thayer's way.

While Lee did not have a chance to originate any major changes while at West Point, he did oversee the expansion of the curriculum from four years to five, though he did not originate the plan. Generally the few improvements he tried to make fell flat. Something as simple as redesigning the cadet's dress hats to make them more comfortable and practical proved to be too complicated for him to complete. For years the students had complained about the top-heavy headgear, which were uncomfortable in general and, since they were made out of black leather, tended to bake cadets' skulls during summer dress parades. Though Lee had new designs created and constructed, his efforts went nowhere. He did succeed, however, in changing the interpretation of one West Point regulation. Previously, a cadet had to accumulate 200 demerits in one year in order to face expulsion. Lee noticed that this meant that many boys paid little attention to the rules until they reached the 190s, and he therefore altered the rule to say they would face serious discipline upon accumulating 100 demerits in a six-month period.

During the spring of 1853, the family faced a tragedy. Mary Custis, whom Lee held in the highest respect and was, indeed, one of his spiritual role models, had suffered declining health in recent months. One day in April she complained of a headache, but seemed fine. The next day, she took a significant turn for the worse and her doctor told the family to expect the end soon. The telegrams went out, and Mary Lee left West Point immediately to be with her mother. She arrived in time for the funeral on April 27.

His mother-in-law's death deeply moved Lee and seemed to put him in mind of other, bigger issues. Though his duties at West Point prevented him from traveling to Arlington, he wrote Mary and his children, trying once again to parent and comfort from a distance. The truths of Christianity and his confidence in Mary Custis's faith left him with no worries for her. He was more concerned about his family's grief and his own. "The more I think of our irreparable loss the greater is my grief . . . ," he said. "Not for her. She has gone from all trouble, Care & Sorrow [*sic*] to a happy immortality." Mary and the younger children remained at Arlington to comfort her distraught father until Lee arrived that summer.

The Sunday after Lee finally joined the rest of his family at Arlington, he presented himself for confirmation in the Episcopal Church along with his daughters Mary and Anne. The presiding minister, Bishop John Johns, laid his hands on their heads in blessing and prayed over them. This was the first time Lee had officially acknowledged his connection to a church in a day and age when most people, whether thoroughgoing Christian or not, joined a congregation as children. This has led to some speculation on the part of historians that this represented a "conversion" for Lee, implying that he had not truly been a practicing Christian before. While this could technically be true, if the right sense of the word "conversion" is assumed, there are better ways to describe Lee's experience. Perhaps the best way to put it would be that his mother-in-law's death brought about a "crystallization" or "realization" in Lee's religious life.

For his part, Lee never seems to have called any of the teachings of the church into serious question. His biological mother, Ann, had done much to inculcate and model the Christian life for him. Mary and her mother were also both stridently evangelical Christians, and had done all they could to increase the church's hold on him. He seems to have accepted the basic points of the faith at an early age, but then very quickly become caught up in the actual *living* of his life on this earth rather than theorizing about what life in the next would be like. As many before and after him have done, he apparently deferred serious thought on those issues until later. As he moved through his forties and realized that his life was in all likelihood more than half over, he began looking at many things more carefully, from his own accomplishments to his conduct as a father to his relationship with God. Mary Custis's death brought all of this into focus, clarifying the issues for Lee. It reminded him of the need to not only pass along his religion to his children, but also to take a more active role in it himself.

If there was a religious theme in Lee's life that most impacted his character, it would be the idea of sin and redemption. From his letters, it is clear that he particularly felt the heavy burden of sin and human imperfection. He knew how far short he had fallen of living a life in which he had done no harm, but he always felt obligated to try again. This sense of his shortcomings led to frustration as he could never reach his own standards, let along those of God, by himself. In fact, as Emory Thomas put it, "Had not the church taught the doctrine of original sin [the idea that all humans are inherently evil and sinful, and therefore in need of salvation], Lee would have invented it." Salvation through belief in Jesus Christ balanced out the equation. Lee believed that he owed God his best efforts to live as perfect a life as he could and in return, God through the person of Christ would grant him grace for his shortcomings. As a result, Lee did his duty—to God, to his family, to his country—and in return God offered him freedom from the intolerable guilt the knowledge of his sins brought him. Lee only sought to deepen his religion from this point until the end of his life.

One advantage to West Point was that it kept Lee in contact with Scott. He also interacted quite a bit with Jefferson Davis, a senator from Mississippi who served as secretary of war. It was probably Scott's influence that brought about Lee's departure into another, drastically different assignment. As the United States continued its inexorable push west, it came into increasing conflict with various American Indian tribes in the Southwest. In Texas in particular, the Comanche had attacked a number of settlements and the people there were pleading for government protection. In 1854–1855, Congress organized four new regiments to respond to the problem, two of infantry and two of cavalry. In the spring of 1855, Davis appointed Lee second in command of one of the cavalry regiments.

This was a drastic departure from anything that Lee had yet experienced. Up to that point in his career, he had been an engineer, scout, and adviser, but he had never commanded men in the field directly. The shift from the "staff" to the "line" would be significant. It would also mean that Lee would be leaving his family again to join his unit in Texas.

As Lee closed his accounts in and around West Point, he could look back on his time there with some little satisfaction. If he had not brought about drastic change, neither had he committed an error so grievous that it would mark his career indelibly. Actually, he received positive reviews from his peers. Still, Lee no doubt looked on his departure from the post with likely no less relief than he had upon emerging from the Pedregal unscathed.

Lee's time in Texas was not the most productive period of his life. He served as second in command to Albert Sydney Johnston in the Second U.S. Cavalry. The unit had been posted to Ft. Mason, about 100 miles north and slightly west of San Antonio. When Lee arrived, Johnston immediately gave him command of two squadrons of cavalry and sent him another 100 miles north to Camp Cooper, where Lee would try to keep the peace between reservation Comanche, a large settlement of Comanche that had left the reservation, and the white settlers in the area. Camp Cooper itself was little more than a collection of tents on the hot Texas prairie near the Clear Fork of the Brazos River.

Lee's views on race began to become more defined during this time. Like many others during the period, Lee believed that certain societies were more advanced than others, and he praised or criticized them accordingly. Of course, Lee placed his own people group, white Southerners, at the top of the proverbial pile. He had disliked the Mexicans, but he respected some of the things they had done and built. Therefore, while he placed them below white Americans in his unwritten scheme of civilization, he did not disdain them totally. The Comanche were another matter entirely. During his time in Texas, he did his best to work with them in order to keep the peace, but he disliked them intensely. He saw them as little better than animals, arguing that "Their paint & ornaments make them more hideous than nature made them & the whole race is extremely uninteresting." While it is obviously premature to suggest that Lee saw the matter as a question of "evolution"—Charles Darwin would not publish his *On the Origin of Species* until 1859—Lee did believe that some cultures were more progressive than others. He did not hesitate to judge those that he did not feel had progressed quickly enough.

Lee once led an expedition out into the Texas countryside after a group of Comanche that had embarked on a raid, but had no real success catching them. He simply did not know the methods necessary to be effective in this type of policing action, and was no match for the Comanche on their own land. One group of Lee's troopers did catch a small group and in the ensuing fight killed two warriors and captured one woman, but Lee's own detachment saw nothing but open prairie.

Lee's other significant pastime, apart from riding through the countryside in search of Indians he never saw, was serving on various courts martial. The massive respect he had earned in the service and his technical availability as a second in command recommended Lee for the job. As a result, while he was stationed in Texas, the army dragged Lee across hundreds of miles in the space of about six months, from fall 1856 through spring 1857. He heard hundreds of hours of tedious argument and exposition during that time about cases that held no real interest for him. Ironically, several times he finished one court martial, traveled 100 or more miles back to Camp Cooper, only to receive immediate orders to proceed to another court martial several hundred miles away in another direction. As he wrote sarcastically to a friend, "Truly, there is no rest for the wicked."

Meanwhile, Lee's woes on the home front continued to mount. Though Custis had graduated West Point and was starting to make his way through the army, the ever troublesome Rooney was having serious problems with his studies at Harvard. Lee wrangled with Rooney in his letters, trying to impart some good sense to his son, and worried that he might not see Custis again before he died due to conflicting deployments. Worse, Mary was slowly succumbing to some form of rheumatic disease, most likely arthritis, and faced a general decline in health. Every summer she traveled to various spas and mineral springs, but their salutary effects never seemed to last long. Though she hid the fact from Lee until his next homecoming, she already could not walk without crutches. This led Lee to the sobering realization that she would not be able to follow him on his wanderings anymore, even if the army posted him to a more congenial location. Rooney finally left Harvard and joined the army, a relief to Lee, but then Rooney became engaged to a woman Lee worried was too fragile to handle the stress of military life. As a result, Lee's deployment became both a curse and a blessing: He was able to avoid dealing with the stresses of home on a daily basis, but felt guilty and disconnected when he dealt with those problems from a distance.

As the country moved closer and closer to war with itself, Lee could not avoid hearing about the political controversies, even out in Texas, and they began to provoke reactions in him. Of course, by the time word reached him through the newspapers, it was already at least two weeks old. The events of "Bleeding Kansas" would certainly have drawn his attention, as free and slave governments both struggled for control of a state not far away. Politically, when the Whigs had self-destructed in the election of 1856, Lee had lost his only national party affiliation, but he was still at heart a Whig and a federalist. He respected states' rights, but he believed in the general primacy of the national government. This was, after all, the government he had faithfully served for more than 25 years, his idol Washington had founded, and his father had fought to establish.

This dedication would soon come into conflict with another: his cultural/social connections to Virginia. Lee was a Virginian through and through, and that demanded precedence over everything else. In Lee's mind, the North, particularly the abolitionist movement, was to blame for the controversies he saw in the papers. He believed that they had offended the South by attempting to forcibly amend its institutions and culture. While Lee was no apologist for slavery, he felt that it was the South's business what it did with its "peculiar institution" and the people held in bondage by it. The only answer to the problem, then, would be for the North to apologize, redress its wrongs, and leave the South alone. This left Lee holding the ends of two increasingly exclusive propositions, and for the moment he did not seriously try to reconcile them. It seemed, though, that the country was on course to force him to make a choice.

On October 10, 1857, the Lee family faced another massive shock as George Washington Parke Custis died at Arlington after contracting pneumonia. He left behind him three plantations totaling over 5,000 acres and the more than 150 slaves who worked them. His will awarded Lee a small plot of land in Washington, D.C. and the massive responsibility of serving as executor. Parke Custis gave Mary the right to live at Arlington for the rest of her life, but left actual ownership of it and his other properties to his male grandchildren, providing substantial cash inheritances for his female grandchildren. He also ordered all of his slaves emancipated as soon as these provisions were carried out successfully or in five years, whichever came first.

Unfortunately, as Parke Custis had fancied himself a writer, artist, and public speaker, he had relied mostly on his status and inherited wealth to get by in life. For years he had taken no direct role in the running of his own affairs, leaving all those details to various managers and overseers with whom he rarely checked. The result was an unmitigated mess, one that his son-in-law now had to sort out. Lee secured leave from Texas and when he arrived home in spring 1858, he found things in a deplorable state. Parke Custis had been heavily in debt and had not maintained any of his plantations properly. When Lee tried to rent out some of the facilities to start raising money to pay debts and fulfill the terms of the will, he found the facilities in such poor condition that he would have to pay two years of rent up front just to put them back into working order. "Light Horse Harry's" poor example had inspired Lee to take scrupulous care of his finances, and over the years he had accumulated a solid financial foundation as a result. He would now have to spend a significant amount of that cleaning up the mess his father-in-law had now left him.

By default, Lee had now become a significant slaveholder for the first time in his life. Slavery was, of course, a normal part of Lee's life and had always been. He and his family had owned servants who attended them as cooks, cleaners, and so forth, but this was the first time that Lee had been forced to manage a large slave workforce. The job was made more difficult by the fact that word of the emancipation provision in the will had leaked out, leaving most of the slaves with the impression that they were to be set free immediately, an idea encouraged by several abolitionists who came over from Washington D.C. and, according to some accounts, suggested the slaves rise up. When Lee explained that they could face up to five more years of enslavement, the slaves took it as a betrayal and several did rebel, though there was no general uprising. Lee had the dissenters forcibly restrained and eventually sent elsewhere. The rest worked, but only very grudgingly. Word of this leaked into the abolitionist press in the form of several letters that exaggerated the situation, but Lee refused to write responses in his defense.

Lee did not prove to be a very successful slaveholder at Arlington. His tendency to avoid conflict and positive abhorrence for outright torture meant that there were some "effective" methods of punishment that he simply would never employ. He preferred to try to win his slaves to his side through the use of kindness and comfort. While he may have had some success in other circumstances, with Parke Custis's former slaves very conscious of the fact that their freedom was due them, they remained unwilling workers. Lee himself professed a strong desire to grant them that freedom, but felt he must see through the other provisions of the will first and for that he needed the slaves' work.

Lee did not like the idea of slavery, and called it an "evil" to both blacks and whites. He believed that slavery should be destroyed, thereby freeing civilization as whole from its corrupting influences. This was definitely a more enlightened view of the situation than that espoused by many Southerners, the more radical of whom were by this time presenting slavery as a positive good and pushing for its expansion. In this, Lee mirrored the Founding Fathers in that he wanted to see slavery put on the course of ultimate extinction, but did not think it could be ended summarily.

Unfortunately, some of Lee's subsequent defenders have exaggerated the extent of his abolitionism in an attempt to absolve him of moral guilt. Lee may have seen slavery more clearly than most of his contemporaries, but overall he still shared many of their views. Lee saw blacks as inferior and placed them below Mexicans but above Comanche in his racial hierarchy. He took a very paternalistic view of slavery, thinking of it as a sort of "painful discipline" that would result in the advancement of the African race that would "lead them to better things." He believed abolition would occur, but only after God worked it through "slow influences." While he wanted to advance the cause of "final abolition" with "all the aid of our prayers & all justifiable means in our power" he did not foresee that day as coming soon. God Himself would bring about its end, and, as Lee noted, to God "two thousand years are but a Single day." However much Lee might wax eloquent on the ultimate evil of slavery, in terms of day-to-day life, he successfully lived with the moral contradiction of owning other human beings, much as fellow Virginian Thomas Jefferson had.

Cleaning up Parke Custis's mess took time. Unfortunately no one else seemed qualified to handle the job. Mary was an only child, and even in the best of health would not have been suited to facing the massive problem. Lee had to repeatedly ask for extensions on his leave, which Scott granted, leaving him absent from his unit for more than two years. During that time, Lee wrestled with the question of whether to quit the army altogether. He had said before and afterward that he would much prefer a quiet life of farming with his family to moving about with the military. Here, of course, was a perfect chance to make that happen. In the end, he decided to stay in the army.

Lee's presence so close to Washington helped ensure that he would be swept up into one of the most famous series of events leading to the Civil War. John Brown was an abolitionist crusader who had most recently led a militia in Kansas, where he had considerably added to its "bloody" reputation with his Pottawattamie Creek Massacre. Brown was a radical's radical, who believed that an end to slavery was not only worth arguing for, but also killing and dying for. As things began to settle down out West, Brown hatched an even more ambitious plan: Start a slave revolt that would grow into an army, an army he could lead against the Southern states in order to secure the freedom of all black Americans. That his ambitious plan had no practical chance of succeeding did not seem to concern Brown, and he was able to sell the idea to six wealthy abolitionists who agreed to bankroll him.

On October 16, 1859, Brown led an armed contingent of about 20 men, including several of his own sons, away from the Maryland farmhouse he was using as his base of operations. Their target was the arsenal at Harpers Ferry, Virginia (now West Virginia). Harpers Ferry was one of only two places in the entire country where the United States could manufacture modern rifled firearms. Brown took the facility with no real trouble and captured some notable hostages, including Lewis W. Washington, a cousin of George. He then announced his success and waited for the slave recruits to pour in. Unfortunately for Brown, the slaves knew his plan was suicidal, even if he did not. No slaves came to join Brown's rebellion.

Word of the attack quickly reached Washington, though the initial descriptions of what was going on were inflated beyond all reason. According to some reports, as many as 3,000 crazed abolitionists had seized the arsenal and were out to start a slave revolt that could lead to massive slaughter. First Lieutenant James Ewell Brown Stuart (called J.E.B., for short) happened to be in the War Department on October 17 and, when Secretary of War John B. Floyd determined to send for Lee, Stuart immediately volunteered to fetch him. Stuart had been a friend of Custis Lee's at West Point and Lee knew him well. Though Stuart was better known for his love of show, he was already an experienced cavalry officer with intelligent, well-developed instincts. Stuart found Lee that morning, working in his civilian clothes at Arlington. Lee left immediately, without changing into his uniform.

Since almost all of the army had been posted to the frontier, Floyd had been able to scrounge up only one company of marines and assorted Maryland militia. Lee ordered these to move on Harpers Ferry via railroad immediately. He and Stuart, who had offered to serve as Lee's second in command, followed as quickly as they could. Lee ordered the troops to wait for him outside town until he joined them.

When Lee and Stuart arrived at about 10 P.M., they got their first relatively sure explanation of what had taken place earlier. When the townspeople had learned what had happened, they had armed themselves and called out the Virginia militia. They attacked Brown's group, and the fight developed into a running street battle. Several of the insurgents had been killed, others escaped, and the few that remained had fled to a brick building on the arsenal grounds that housed firefighting equipment. The locals had vaguely surrounded the building and were shooting at anything near it that moved, including a few things that did not (as evidenced by their angry desecration of the bodies of a few of Brown's men who still lay in the open).

Lee immediately ordered the citizens of Harpers Ferry and their militia allies to return home, and then he placed the Maryland militia he had brought with him in prominent places surrounding the building. He wanted to block off all escape and for the trapped men to see him do so to make sure they knew the hopelessness of their position. He then had to decide how to end the situation with the least risk to the hostages. By the early morning of October 18, he had arrived at a plan. Lee had no intention of engaging in any extended negotiations. Either the fighters would surrender immediately or he would storm the building. He wrote a note to that effect for Stuart to deliver and pulled together an attack party from the marines when the militia declined the honor.

The people of Harpers Ferry were obviously more excited by the prospect of watching the end of the siege than they were awed by Lee's insistence that they leave; when Stuart advanced to the engine house under a flag of truce at 7:00 A.M., more than 2,000 were in attendance. Brown met Stuart at the door, heard the note, and when he tried to dicker for time, Stuart stepped back and gave the signal for the attack to begin. Though the marines had trouble with the door at first, they soon broke a large hole in it and forced their way inside. A few marines and insurgents were wounded and killed, but the hostages escaped unscathed. Brown himself was wounded seriously, but survived.

Brown became a sensation after he was wounded and did far more to further the cause of immediate abolition (and civil war) through his death than he ever could have through life. He had touched on the greatest fear of white slaveholders: slave revolt. The idea that the slaves might one day rise up and violently resist their masters, as Nat Turner had, was never far from anyone's mind. Even Lee, who considered his sympathy to be with the slaves, remarked on this to Rooney, stating "I trust you will so gain the affection of your people that they will not wish to do you any harm." Large-scale slave revolt could mean the deaths of tens of thousands of men, women, and children of both races, as had been demonstrated in places like Haiti and the Dominican Republic. Brown had tried to implement this, and it frightened many in the South into taking a more radical point of view. Worse, in the North Brown was increasingly lauded as a hero for being willing to strike such a blow. Most in the North had not heard the gory details of Brown's actions in Kansas, nor did they really understand what the success of his plan in Harpers Ferry would have meant in terms of sheer bloodshed. Brown's behavior at his trial and eventual execution only increased his popularity and that of his cause. While historians know that abolitionists were still far from a majority in the North, to a terrified South at the time, that fact was not so apparent.

Lee, still anticipating orders to return to Texas, wrote a report for the War Department about his role in the crisis and was part of the guard that watched for abolitionist interference at Brown's hanging. He later testified before Congress in early 1860, but had nothing substantial to add to the tale. Lee's role in the situation had been significant, and he had once again handled himself well. He responded to the unexpected call to action without hesitation. He moved his troops to the scene quickly, but was careful not to commit them until he had a clearer idea of what had happened. Once he knew, he acted decisively to protect the civilians and hostages while eliminating the threat. Harpers Ferry also demonstrated an important aspect of Lee's military character: his willingness to take chances. Lee would take calculated risks, as he did with the lives of the hostages. Lucky for them, Lee's gambles had a way of paying off.

With Lee's decision's to stay in the army, he knew it would only be a matter of time before he would be sent to his next post. He had expected to receive orders to deploy as far back as October 1859, but they were delayed until February 1860. Lee was to take command of the Department of Texas, and would report to San Antonio to take over his duties. So, once again, Lee left Mary and the girls to follow the military life. This time, though, the country he had served so long seemed ready to fall apart, and he would soon have to choose: the nation or Virginia.

Chapter 3

OBSCURITY, PESSIMISM, AND FAILURE

With the Civil War looming, Lee returned to Texas in 1860 and took up his post at San Antonio, but his time there proved short-lived and rather pointless. There were much bigger issues afoot than the small, often petty disagreements he mediated for the army. He could not know it then, but in only a year he would be in the field, in rebellion against the United States, in command of tens of thousands of Confederate troops. He would experience failure and embarrassment in the beginning and only later a taste of the success for which he is better known.

Lee spent the majority of his time in command of the Department of Texas dealing with bureaucratic and clerical issues, with grievances from the troops, and overseeing the ever exciting courts martial. When Mexican bandit Juan Cortinas raised a small but well-armed band and raided the settlements around Brownsville, Lee led a cavalry detachment after him. He traveled hither and yon through the arid countryside, but, like the Comanche, Cortinas proved too wily for Lee to catch. Lee did act as a sort of ambassador between the Texans on the border and Mexican authorities who were, in theory, also pursuing Cortinas. In that role, he succeeded in bringing about a semblance of peace in the vicinity. Cortinas's band was dispersed by the pursuit and he ceased to be a problem, at least for a time.

About this time, Lee also had to face the reality of his own humanity, if not mortality. He spent a notable amount of time during this tour complaining of illness. This was a relatively new experience for him, since he had enjoyed robust health for most of his life. Most of Lee's biographers only record one or two cases prior to this point where he had been laid up sick, unable to travel or perform his duties. Lee now found that the ailments were more frequent and also more constant when they occurred. He complained of a continuing cold and a pain in his right arm that he wrote off as rheumatic. While it is of course impossible to tell, some of these aches and pains may have been the first signs of the heart problems that would help kill him in about a decade.

While Lee found relief from the sweltering Texas summer when temperatures fell that autumn, the national controversies around him seemed to be heating up. Several Southern states had already pledged themselves to secede from the Union if "Black Republican" Abraham Lincoln won that year's presidential election. They had made threats like this before, and many in the North doubted their sincerity. People on both sides of the Mason-Dixon Line expected another round of vicious negotiations that would culminate in yet another compromise. This time, however, things were different. The actions of John Brown and the abolitionists on one side and a cadre of equally radical Southern speakers and writers called Fire-eaters on the other had brought things to a fever pitch. Worse, the debate had reached a point where compromise might not be possible. The central theme of the Republican Party was that slavery must not be allowed to expand into the territories. Southerners demanded that slavery be allowed to expand where it would. There really was no middle ground on which a compromise could find footing: slavery would either expand or not.

All speculation stopped after Lincoln's election when in December 1860 South Carolina, the most radical state on the slavery question, seceded from the Union. In January, a string of other Deep South states followed South Carolina's example. Of more immediate importance for Lee, Texas voted for secession on February 1, 1861. The rest of the seceded states met in Montgomery, Alabama on February 4 to form the Confederate States of America. Though Texas was a bit late, when its delegates reached Montgomery, it also signed on with the new nation. Virginia and the other border states tried to keep everyone calm. Many in those states knew that if war came, it would come first and foremost to their doorsteps, and the idea that their homes could be visited and destroyed by the armies made them more circumspect.

Lee thought that the idea of secession made little sense, for more than one reason. He did not believe that it was constitutional, and for him that was a serious consideration. At the time, both sides of the political aisle believed the Constitution should be read as an actual body of specific laws that should be followed as opposed to the more modern interpretation (pioneered in the 20th century by Oliver Wendell Holmes Jr.) that sees it as a set of general guidelines that mean whatever courts want them to mean. He also did not believe secession was practical. While some Southern politicians had offered to wipe up all the blood spilled as a result of their departure from the Union with a handkerchief, Lee knew that "Secession is nothing but revolution." He expected some sort of hostilities, and probably knew that there would be significant bloodshed. If the South tried to secede, then the federal government would try to stop them. If that happened, the South would have to raise an army to repel any forces sent from Washington. So, assuming the South had to fight a war in order to insure that they could "peacefully" secede, how would that be any different from a revolution?

Out in Texas, Lee and his fellow officers had to decide what they would do. Lee seemed ambivalent. He was saddened at the prospect of the dismemberment of the nation that he had served so faithfully for so long. Still, he felt that the North had provoked the situation and that "a Union that can only be maintained by swords and bayonets . . . has no charm for me." Now that it came to it, his loyalty to Virginia dominated his preference for the Union. He remarked several times, with only slight variations, that he hoped to return to Arlington where he could take up planting again and quietly retire from the army. If Virginia decided to secede, though, Lee would place himself at his home state's disposal. "[I]f she secedes (though I do not believe in secession as a constitutional right, nor that there is a sufficient cause for revolution), then I will follow my native State with my sword, and, if need be, with my life."

Lee received orders to report to Scott in person and left Texas in the turmoil of secession. He arrived back at Arlington on March 1, 1861. He saw Scott shortly thereafter and learned that he would finally be promoted to the full rank of colonel and given command of the First Cavalry Regiment. More likely, Scott, seeing where the crisis was headed, wanted Lee close to him. By this point in his life, Scott was old and infirm. He suffered from bouts of vertigo and had gained so much weight that he could not mount a horse. That left Scott, still in command of all United States forces, obviously unable to take command in the field, if it came to that. Scott likely hoped to have Lee, his protégé and most trusted man, lead the army in the field while Scott coordinated strategy.

April saw the crisis snowball beyond recovery. Lincoln was sworn in as president on March 4, and he made a point of trying to hold two forts in the South still occupied by Federal forces. The most important of these was Ft. Sumter, which guarded the harbor of Charleston, South Carolina. Charleston was the most radical area of the most radical slave state in the Union. The fort was quickly surrounded by militia and then Confederate troops. When Lincoln tried to resupply the troops stationed there, the newly elected president of the Confederacy, Jefferson Davis, ordered his commander on the scene to open fire on the fort. The bombardment lasted about a day and resulted in no casualties, but the fort surrendered on April 14. Lincoln called for 75,000 volunteers to serve for three months to put down the rebellion, while a slightly more farsighted Davis called for 100,000 to serve for a year.

Four days after Sumter's fall, Lee received two meeting requests, one from Scott and one from Francis P. Blair. Blair was the patriarch of a powerful political family with close ties to Lincoln. Lee obligingly went up to Washington the next day and met with both men. Blair, working for Lincoln at Scott's recommendation, offered Lee command of the Federal army that was then forming in and around Washington. Lee politely declined, once again saying that he could never raise his sword against his native state. The Virginia legislature was at that moment considering secession, and many observers expected it to join the Confederacy. Blair pressed Lee, but Lee refused. Lee then left Blair's house for a much more emotional interview with Scott. Scott also tried to convince Lee to stay with the Union and take command of the army, but Lee stood firm. The bittersweet meeting concluded amiably, and Lee returned to Arlington. He heard the news that Virginia had officially seceded the next day on a trip into Alexandria. That night Mary said she could hear her husband pacing the floor above her, wrestling with his final decision. Just after midnight, Lee took up his pen and wrote an appreciative letter of resignation to Scott. He came downstairs shortly thereafter to see his wife. "Well, Mary," he said, "the question is settled."

The political scramble for command on both sides began almost everywhere at once. The United States army had been only about 15,000 strong when the war opened, and many of those men had left to follow their states as Lee had. The Confederates were, of course, creating an army out of almost nothing. That meant that there would be hundreds of positions for officers opening up quite literally overnight, and people with dreams of martial glory or political success maneuvered to fill them. A soldier of Lee's stature did not have to engage in any of this sort of begging for command, though. Lee had a towering reputation in the army and in Virginia, and it would only be a matter of time before he would receive an offer from someone.

It came almost instantly. Judge John Robertson of Richmond sent word that Governor John Letcher wanted Lee to come to Richmond. Lee left Arlington on April 22, 1861, never to return. Letcher offered Lee command of all Virginia's military forces, army and navy, with the rank of major general. This time, Lee agreed. He had the opportunity to turn down the command, to return home and raise his corn, but he chose to take up arms with Virginia. Lee was at heart a Virginian and a soldier. Now he now could be both at once.

The army and navy Lee presided over existed only on paper. Though the Virginia militia was approximately the same size as the prewar U.S. army had been, it was, as were most of the country's militias, more concerned with socializing than with making war. When pulling his forces together, Lee knew he would have to rely on volunteers, but as much as possible, he placed those volunteers under the command of seasoned regulars. Many Virginia officers (though not all) had joined their state, and he set the veterans he had to drilling and organizing forces. He took full advantage of the Virginia Military Institute (VMI) and sent its professors and cadets across the state to help with training. Lee knew that due to Virginia's proximity to Washington, D.C., the Union army would most likely strike there first. Hence Lee designated assembly and training sites near key defensive positions. Knowing that the York and James Rivers both offered excellent invasion routes, he ordered his old superior and friend Andrew Talcott to build defensive positions along both. In a few weeks, Lee had organized more than 40,000 troops and seized dozens of artillery pieces, which he rapidly distributed among the various units and coastal/river defense batteries.

Lee's family scattered as a result of secession, throwing themselves into the service of their new nation without any serious reservation. Custis and Rooney soon donned the uniform again, though young Rob remained at the University of Virginia for a time. Rob would eventually join the Rockbridge Artillery and later encountered his father several times during the war. In a very short time, it became clear that Mary and the girls must leave Arlington, which would no doubt be occupied by Union forces. United States troops took the house shortly after they left. Most of the girls moved about, living with friends and family, though Mildred stayed with Mary. Mary was kept on the move too, outraged by the idea that her precious Arlington had been desecrated by Yankees. She never seemed to move as far or as quickly as her husband wanted.

At this point, Lee had not acquired the god-like reputation that he later would, and was simply one more man in uniform, albeit a distinguished one. People had high expectations for what he would accomplish, but he did not command the massive presence he would by war's end, and soldiers' morale did not rise by default when he came by, as it would in 1865. In fact, Lee seemed to be somewhat pessimistic about the South's chances. He knew that the North would not simply let secession happen and that it possessed a population and resources vastly superior to the South. Lee would risk his life for Virginia because it was his duty, but he did not spin any wild tales of easy victory or Yankees whipped with cornstalks. This disturbed a number of pundits, who complained of Lee's grim outlook to Davis and Letcher.

In late May, the Confederate congress voted to move the government to Richmond, and Governor Letcher transferred control of Virginia's state forces to the Confederacy. This left Lee without an army or post. Lee did not know what he would be expected to do next. In the meantime, he remained in Richmond with President Davis. Since the two men had worked together closely while Lee had been superintendant of West Point and Davis the secretary of war, they knew each other well. Davis trusted Lee, increasingly sought his advice on military matters, and, as events progressed, he used him as an unofficial adviser and staff officer. Given that most people still expected a short, easy war, Lee interjected a sense of realism into Davis's discussions that would have otherwise been absent. After the First Battle of Bull Run on July 21, many Southerners thought that the war was essentially over. Lee continued to advise caution, arguing that the war would be bloody and had only just begun.

As Lee and Davis continued to face the dangers of eastern Virginia, they also had significant problems with the western part of the state. In general, the mountainous portions of the Confederacy tended to be more pro-Union than the piedmont or coastal regions. Slaveholders in the mountains were few and far between, given that those areas did not lend themselves to large plantations. Western Virginia, eastern Tennessee, northern Alabama, and northern Georgia all harbored significant numbers of Unionists who did not necessarily plan on accepting the Confederacy quietly. In July 1861, Union general George B. McClellan had attacked the rickety Confederate defenses in what would later become West Virginia and shattered them. Only the fact that McClellan had returned east in order to start building what would become the Army of the Potomac in the wake of Bull Run had prevented a complete Confederate rout in the area. In McClellan's place, William Rosecrans had taken command and was preparing to renew the offensive. Davis dispatched Lee to the northwest to oversee operations there and hopefully undo some of the damage McClellan had wrought.

Lee had never directed a battle before taking his first active command at Valley Mountain. He did have his reputation to live up to, however. People all over the Confederacy knew him as perfection incarnate, the son of revolutionary hero "Light Horse Harry" Lee. From a historical perspective, these kinds of expectations were totally unrealistic and even in the best circumstances, Lee would have had trouble living up to them.

The situation was anything but ideal. At about the time Lee arrived to coordinate operations, Virginia did its best impression of a rainforest. One observer wrote that over the course of about 40 days, it rained all but 3. At the time, most of America's roads were still unpaved, many little better than trails, and that sort of weather turned them into mires that made movement almost impossible. An unseasonable cold then set in and many of the Confederates in the area fell ill. At one point, Lee speculated that the sick could have made up an army by themselves, if only they could move.

The officers on duty did nothing to help the situation. The main commander at Valley Mountain, where Lee at first hoped to take the offensive, was William W. Loring, a one-armed, ornery, and self-centered Mexican War veteran. He commanded approximately 14,000 men, only about 10,000 of whom were fit for duty. Loring resented Lee's presence and gave him a minimum of cooperation, spending his time in a never-ending accumulation of supplies for an offensive that always seemed just about to start. The other two commanders in the area were both former governors of Virginia: John B. Floyd and Henry Wise. Each led a smaller force to the west, and they loathed each other. Wise seemed to have better military instincts, at least in terms of geography, but he had no sense of military discipline. He took even legitimate orders from clear superiors as suggestions to be considered and then almost inevitably protested. Floyd was a bit better at taking orders, but he had no military instincts whatsoever. Neither man really had any business leading an army.

Lee's style of command made things even worse. He had recently been appointed a full general with the Confederacy, third in rank behind Samuel Cooper (Davis's chief of staff) and his old commander, Albert Sydney Johnston. As such, he technically outranked everyone else in the field. Unfortunately, for some reason he never really exercised his authority by taking firm control of affairs. He worked mainly as an adviser and tried to reason with Loring, Floyd, and Wise. He saw his role as a coordinator and enabler, hoping to make it easier for them to do their jobs. That might have worked if Lee had been dealing with more capable officers. Instead, respecting their opinions and prerogatives only gave them free reign to ignore him. Worse, Lee had still not shed himself of his nearly pathological fear of confrontation. He would sometimes let himself be railroaded by lesser men with louder mouths and worse tempers—men like Loring. Later, when Lee had begun to take on legendary proportions, the negative effects of his command style became somewhat muted as fewer and fewer people would stand up to him or disregard him, but at this point in his career with the Confederacy, it contributed to the fiasco that followed.

Lee stepped into western Virginia intent on assuming the offensive. Rosecrans's line was long and thin, and Lee believed he could break it somewhere. He first worked with Loring at Valley Mountain, near Huttonsville. When Loring resisted Lee's advice and stalled, Lee moved his headquarters farther away rather than deal with the situation. Even when Loring felt like cooperating, the weather usually did not. Finally, after receiving a key piece of information, Loring and Lee agreed to attack the Union position on nearby Cheat Mountain. A force would surprise the Federals on the mountain and once they had swept it clear of resistance, the rest of the army could advance and seize Huttonsville. It was a good plan that should have worked well.

On the morning of September 12, 1861, despite another punishing rain storm, all of the Confederates were in position. The attack force on Cheat Mountain was to go in first, and the sound of their fighting would signal the others to advance. Lee and Loring waited all morning for the guns to echo, but they heard nothing but silence. The day passed with no action. What had happened? The leader of the attack column, Colonel Albert Rust, had gotten his troops into place, but had the unfortunate success of capturing a few Federals early that morning. His prisoners had spun wild tales of a supposedly massive force on the crest of Cheat Mountain. Rust had crept forward himself, and, being completely inexperienced, had "confirmed" the report by entirely miscalculating the number of troops he saw. As a result, he had called off the attack. Without Rust to start them off, the rest of the army sat there, shivering in the cold rain. Loring eventually retreated, leaving the area in Federal hands.

Lee acknowledged the defeat, as did the army. They had suffered bitterly during the campaign and emerged with nothing to show for it. Lieutenant Walter Taylor, on Lee's staff for the whole war, remarked that he never again saw soldiers suffer as they had during this campaign. To go through so much only to find that they had made no difference whatsoever sent the soldiers' morale plummeting. In response, Lee offered the sobering response that "We must try again."

He did so with Floyd and Wise, and experienced similar results. On September 10, while Lee had been waiting for nothing to happen at Cheat Mountain, Rosecrans had attacked Floyd at Carnifax Ferry. Floyd had appealed to Wise for help, and Wise had refused to send any. Floyd held on through the day, but retreated after dark, thinking he faced much longer odds than he actually did. Floyd tried repeatedly to order Wise to join him in his advanced position, but Wise either offered excuses or simply ignored him each time. Wise preferred to have Floyd join him at a position farther south that he believed (rightly) was the better for defense. So the pair remained locked in a contest of wills, accomplishing nothing of significance.

Lee tried in vain to convince the two men to work together. He backed Floyd against Wise, saying that Wise's responses amounted to insubordination. On the other hand, Lee agreed with Wise that his position on Sewell Mountain was the stronger, and he suggested that Floyd retire there. Floyd responded by ignoring the chain of command and bringing the situation straight to Davis. Davis removed Wise by calling him back east. Wise once again tried to disobey his orders, later stating that he only followed them because Lee told him to do so.

With all that time wasted, Lee convinced Floyd to pull the two forces together in an attempt to bait Rosecrans into an attack. In early October, it looked like Rosecrans might oblige, but he suddenly withdrew, leaving Floyd and Lee sitting where they were. Lee remained in the area for another three weeks before finally returning to Richmond. Behind him, most of western Virginia was still firmly in Federal control. He once again took up his role as Davis's unofficial adviser.

Lee's return to Richmond was accompanied with much disappointment and not a little mockery. Wise actually owned a significant interest in the Richmond *Enquirer* and his son was one of the editors. One of Floyd's aides during the campaign had been John M. Daniel, editor of the Richmond *Examiner*. At first they had given Lee some positive publicity, insisting that the campaign had been an unqualified success. As a clear picture of defeat slowly emerged from the confusion and spin, they turned on Lee. The army began venting its frustrations about the campaign, often making Lee the scapegoat for Loring, Wise, and Floyd. As the absurdly high expectations came crashing down, Lee was transformed, almost overnight, from Virginia's foremost soldier into

"Granny Lee," a man supposedly so quiet and refined that he was not capable of doing what needed to be done.

Though frustrating in the short run, the campaign proved useful to Lee. Many commanders in the war had one or two early moments of embarrassment, and they had to hope that they came at the right time. Ulysses S. Grant had the Battle of Belmont. Jackson's early Valley maneuvers were certainly less than stellar. These failures were an important part of their learning process, but they had to occur when relatively few people were paying attention. If they lost too prominent a battle, they would simply be shuffled off the field and not given a chance to redeem themselves. Lee's attempt to save western Virginia had failed, but not so prominently that Davis or the rest of the Confederate government lost faith in him. It gave him a chance to really experience campaigning in the Civil War, and he learned quite a bit from it. He learned how to work with troop morale, the need to maintain the offensive, and how important it was to finish what his army started.

One lesson he did not learn was the necessity of dealing with problem officers directly and clearly. For the rest of the war, he approached these issues with far more subtlety than he probably should have. He would never confront an officer to his face. Instead, if someone caused trouble, Lee simply had Davis transfer him out of his army. That led to problems with some of his commanders trying to take advantage of Lee's apparent lack of backbone and, worse, the Confederate western theater tended to become a dumping ground for those who failed in the east. Given that the North's above average commanders were already emerging in the west, this was a recipe for ultimate disaster.

Lee emerged from the campaign with one more important addition to his staff/family. While at Sewell Mountain, a four-year-old stallion named Jeff Davis had caught his attention. The gray horse was powerfully built and impressed Lee. He talked with the owner about buying the animal, but nothing came of it then. A few months later, Lee encountered Jeff Davis, now named Greenbrier, in South Carolina. This time, he did purchase him. Lee renamed him Traveller and rode him for the rest of his life. Traveller eventually became almost as famous as his master.

Lee arrived back in Richmond on Halloween, 1861. About the same time, news reached the Confederates that the Union was fitting out a fleet for a coastal assault. It arrived off Hampton Roads just before Lee returned. The Confederate secretary of war, Judah P. Benjamin, believed that they intended to attack South Carolina, where they could potentially disrupt Confederate communications and establish a refueling base for Union blockade ships farther south. Benjamin created a new department encompassing the coasts of South Carolina, Georgia, and eastern Florida, and he placed Lee in charge.

Lee left Richmond in a hurry on November 6, arriving in Charleston just in time to hear that Port Royal, South Carolina, had fallen to the Federals. To make matters more complicated, Lee's damaged reputation had preceded him, and howls of protest were coming from all over the low country. Davis was actually reduced to writing letters of recommendation for Lee to assuage wounded sensibilities.

Lee toured his department, putting his engineering skills to good use fortifying key ports like Savannah and Charleston. If his charges disliked him, they did not impress him either. Lee found that the first wave of war fever was wearing off as reality sank in. People were beginning to realize that they were indeed in a real war, not just some inspirational story, and that there were other people out there willing to inflict pain, deprivation, and death upon them in order to win the war. Understandably, this made them nervous. As Lee wrote to Custis, "I am dreadfully disappointed at the spirit here. They have all of a sudden realized the asperities of war, in what they must encounter & do not seem prepared for it." Lee tended to confront them with harsh realities, which made them feel no better. His suggestion that Brunswick, Georgia be destroyed and abandoned to the enemy because the Confederacy had no troops to hold it was just one example.

Meanwhile, out West, the Confederacy had already begun to fall apart. One of the Confederacy's greatest assets in the West had been Kentucky. When the war opened, Kentucky had declared itself neutral, banning the troops of both sides from entering the state. Lincoln, convinced that Kentucky's secession would make the war unwinnable, scrupulously observed the provisions. Even though it was technically not a Confederate state, Kentucky's neutrality served the Southern cause well. The state acted as a barrier against Union invasion for the whole length of the long northern border of Tennessee. It was key for the simple reason that the Confederates did not have nearly enough men to guard that much territory. Kentucky protected most of it, greatly limiting Union invasion routes and allowing Davis to concentrate his troops.

All that changed when Davis's friend and West Point crony Leonidas Polk invaded Columbus, Kentucky to build a fort. The Kentucky legislature protested vigorously, and then fell straight into Lincoln's waiting arms. This opened the Confederacy's entire northern frontier in the West to invasion, and Grant did not take long to act on it. In February 1862, Grant took Fts. Henry and Donelson, easily outmaneuvering Gideon Pillow (who had returned from retirement to embarrass himself further), Floyd (fresh from the exile into which Lee sent him), and Simon B. Buckner. This forced Albert Sydney Johnston, commanding in the West, to give up most of Tennessee and retreat into northern Mississippi.

Lee was having some headaches of his own. On December 20, 1861, the Union navy had sunk a flotilla of stone-laden vessels in the middle of the main channel into Charleston Harbor. Ironically, while Lee vented his anger, calling it, "unworthy of any nation," he was himself still in the process of blocking rivers and destroying anything that might be of use to his enemies. Later, on February 7, 1862, 10,000 Federals landed at Roanoke Island, North Carolina. Henry Wise fought a small battle with them the next day and almost immediately surrendered.

The continued antics of Floyd and Wise demonstrate the unfortunate side effect of Lee's preferred approach to dealing with dissent by sending incompetent men elsewhere. Both Floyd and Wise survived Lee to lose battles for the Confederacy in other places. In Floyd's case, he managed to lose one of the key battles of the war, and to do so in such an inept way that historians still regularly and justly ridicule his performance. While these decisions obviously reflect on Davis as much as Lee, if Lee had confronted and dealt with the situation in his own theater, Floyd and Wise might have been able to do less damage to the Confederate cause.

By March 1862, when Davis recalled Lee to Richmond, Lee had taken strong steps toward establishing a firm defensive line in the Deep South. He took a sensible approach and did not try to hold every bit of land at all costs. Instead, he made his defenses match his resources. This groundwork allowed the key ports of Charleston and

Mid-Mississippi Regional Library System
Attala, Holmes, Leake, Montgomery
and Winston Counties

Savannah to hold out against increasing odds until the last days of the war, though Savannah's Ft. Pulaski, built on the foundation Lee had helped lay on Cockspur Island so long before, fell very quickly. Even there Lee's foresight showed, since even though he himself expected Pulaski to stand, he had already established another, closer fort to defend Savannah.

In Richmond, Lee once again occupied a very vague post and was "charged with the conduct of military operations in the army of the Confederacy." No one, including Lee, seemed to have the foggiest idea what that actually meant. Lee had no particular command, and therefore could not issue any orders. In terms of seniority, he may have outranked all but two men, but one of those men, Albert S. Johnston, was in charge of the biggest and ultimately most important theater of the war. All Lee could do was advise the various officers on the plans he thought best, and they could take or leave his suggestions. It may be that Davis, who fancied himself a military genius and planned to exercise real control over his armies, intended Lee to become a sort of second in command. If that was so, Davis never explained that to Lee and it never came to pass.

As Lee whiled away the days and hours on the Southern coast in his old role of engineer, George McClellan had been building his new army outside Washington. In relatively short order, he had taken a disorganized mass of men with no real military experience and turned them into one of the finest looking armies the continent had ever seen. Renamed the Army of the Potomac, McClellan's men would become the main Union fighting force in the eastern theater for the duration of the war, long after McClellan himself had ceased to lead it.

McClellan proved to be excellent at creating armies. He held fine reviews, culled out inferior officers and raised morale to a fever pitch. He loved his men, and they idolized him in return. He proved to be much less adept at actually using his army, however. As the days passed and 1862 grew older, people (President Lincoln foremost among them) began to wonder if McClellan actually intended to do anything at all. When McClellan finally did tentatively advance toward Manassas Junction, the site of the First Battle of Bull Run, he was embarrassed to find no Rebels hiding behind the imposing earthworks and fake cannons scattered about the area.

Shortly thereafter, McClellan finally put forward a plan and acted on it. Invading Virginia from the north presented a number of geographic problems, not the least of which was the rivers that an army would have to cross. The waterways of the Old Dominion generally flowed from west to east, and presented defenders with plenty of opportunity to repel or delay invaders. McClellan hoped to transfer his large army of 100,000 men to Ft. Monroe, Virginia, a Union bastion on the Atlantic coast. From there, he could advance westward toward Richmond up the peninsula formed by the York and James Rivers, both of which would then be protected avenues of supply rather than barriers. Though his plans were delayed somewhat by the ironclad CSS *Virginia*, McClellan began to assemble his men at Ft. Monroe.

Confederate Major General John B. Magruder, an old army officer of Lee's acquaintance, faced McClellan and his vast assembly with only 10,000 men. Though he thought the situation hopeless, he put on a show for McClellan, hoping to keep him occupied. Magruder paraded his men around in front of the Federals, had officers calling out orders to nonexistent regiments, and generally tried to look as busy and teeming as possible. He even had men march out toward Richmond by a hidden path, load into an empty train out in the countryside and then ride it back into his positions so they could visibly unload, only to repeat the process again and again. His antics left the impression that he not only had a large army but that he was receiving constant reinforcements. McClellan fell for it, convinced that Magruder outnumbered him rather than vice versa. Though the Army of the Potomac was already 10 times more powerful than its opponents, McClellan thought that the Confederates had twice his number of men and harassed Lincoln with constant calls for more troops, particularly another 40,000 under Irvin McDowell near Washington. He laid careful siege to Magruder's lines rather than simply marching straight through him, and this bought Richmond the time it needed to respond.

Back in the capital, there was dissent among Davis's advisers. They faced a dire situation on all sides. Grant was pushing them in the West and they continued to lose smaller bastions along the rivers and coasts. Every commander called for more arms and reinforcements, but they had none to send. Now McClellan had arrived on the peninsula with an army so large that the Confederacy had little hope of matching it without drastically weakening other fronts. Lee started calling troops to the capital as fast as he could, but it would take time to assemble the army. The biggest controversy opened on where the best place to face McClellan would be. Lee argued that he should be kept as far from Richmond as possible, and therefore he wanted the decisive battle to be fought out on the peninsula near where Magruder faced McClellan. Lee's old friend Joseph E. Johnston (as distinguished from Albert Sydney, who by now had died at the Battle of Shiloh) had arrived to take command of the army under Magruder. Johnston wanted to retreat to Richmond and fight just outside the city itself. After hours of debate, Davis decided in favor of Lee's approach.

Johnston did not want to concede the point, and a petty complaint about rank complicated the situation further. Johnston had been much more of a politician in the old army than Lee and had achieved the rank of brigadier general, making him Lee's superior officer. He resented the fact that Lee now held more seniority in the Confederate service. When ordered to take the fight to McClellan, Johnston set the pattern for which he would be best known: retreat. Rather than make the best of each situation, Johnston found one reason after another why he could not fight where he was and pulled back. Lee tried to communicate with Johnston and help him, but Johnston did not reciprocate and in general tried to acknowledge Lee as little as possible. He also made little effort to keep Davis informed of what was happening. Soon Johnston would be in front of Richmond, where McClellan *must* be stopped, and, coincidentally, the battle would occur precisely where Johnston had wanted to be all along.

Meanwhile, McDowell and his men lurked in the back of everyone's mind, especially McClellan's. "Little Mac" was convinced that he was so far outnumbered that he *must* have McDowell there in order to have a realistic chance to defeat Johnston. Lee and Davis were worried that if Johnston became too entangled with McClellan, McDowell would advance from the north and they would not be able to oppose him. While still technically without command, Lee dealt with the situation with the help of Thomas J. "Stonewall" Jackson and his small Army of the Valley in the Shenandoah. In another irony, one of Lee's oldest friends was trying to ignore and undercut him while Jackson, probably the Confederacy's most paranoid commander who told no one anything, coordinated with Lee closely.

Jackson had been born to a poor family in what is now West Virginia and was raised by relatives for almost all of his childhood. He attended West Point and managed to pass through sheer willpower, forcing himself to study for hours after other cadets were asleep. His iron discipline became a theme throughout his life and he did not seem to understand why others lacked it. Jackson served with distinction in the Mexican War and the advent of the Civil War had found him a professor of artillery at the Virginia Military Institute in Lexington. Jackson was a staunch Presbyterian who sought the will of God in all things, and also gave God the credit for all of his victories. He was secretive to a fault, but he worked well with Lee. Lee soon found that he could trust Jackson to do his job, and therefore once Lee gave Jackson an assignment, he generally left Stonewall to it.

Lee knew that Lincoln and other Northern politicians were terrified that the South might successfully use the Shenandoah Valley corridor to attack Washington. The valley provided the South with a protected route that opened right into the heart of the Union east, while its western end emerged into the rough terrain of eastern Tennessee, an area of little strategic value. Lee took advantage of this by loosing Jackson to run wild in the valley. When Johnston tried to call Jackson to join him, it was Lee's turn to obstruct, and he quietly manipulated things to not only keep Jackson in the valley, but also support him with more troops. Over the course of May 1862, Jackson assaulted the army of Nathaniel P. Banks, driving him up the valley toward Washington. After one surprise attack had routed Bank's forces near the border with Maryland, Banks tried to rally his men, shouting at one as he ran by, "Good god, man! Don't you love your country?!" The man allegedly replied without breaking stride, "Yes! And I'm trying to get back to it as fast as I can!"

Lincoln, thinking he saw a chance to strike back, ordered two armies to enter the Shenandoah from opposite sides, hoping to cut off Jackson's escape. Taking advantage of his superior knowledge of the ground with a series of hard marches, Jackson managed to inflict embarrassing defeats on both enemies before slipping cleanly away when Lee called him back to Richmond. Jackson very quickly became almost a bogie-like figure in the North, and people seemed to expect him to pop out in front of Washington at any moment. Lincoln recalled McDowell, ordering him to guard the capital against Jackson. McClellan, already paranoid, interpreted this as Lincoln attempting to scuttle the Richmond campaign. From that moment on, McClellan seemed fixated not on taking the Confederate capital, but on retreating his army back out of harm's way.

Johnston finally bestirred himself for an attack, not wanting to let McClellan press him into the city itself. The Battle of Seven Pines/Fair Oaks resulted on May 31, 1862. Necessity had forced McClellan to stretch his army across the Chickahominy River, effectively splitting it in two. He linked the sides with several bridges in his rear. Johnston massed a large force south of the river, hoping to destroy that half of McClellan's army before the other half could come to its aid. Though aided by a deluge that threatened to wipe out the bridges, Johnston's army suffered from inexperience and bungled orders, and the Federals held fast. More important, Johnston rode forward personally to observe and direct the fighting. While there, he had been knocked from his horse by a piece of shrapnel and severely wounded. Though it proved not to be a fatal blow, it would take him months to recover. The fighting cost 6,000 Confederates compared to 5,000 Federals and did not significantly alter the armies' positions.

Johnston's fall and overall failure left Davis in a difficult position. McClellan was still formidable and he was still on Richmond's doorstep. Given the crisis, Davis had to appoint a new commander immediately, and could not wait to call someone from another post. Though he probably seriously considered taking command himself, Davis turned to Lee. Lee assumed command of the forces around Richmond on June 1, 1862, and shortly thereafter gave them the name history would remember: the Army of Northern Virginia.

If the army expected quick action and immediate glorious victories, Lee disappointed them. He disengaged his men and pulled back toward the city, wanting a bit of room where he could reorganize and re-equip. McClellan politely obliged, allowing Lee plenty of time to get ready. Lee combed through his force, ridding himself of incompetent men and replacing them with people he thought could be trusted. The men noted that "Granny Lee" seemed to be living up to his reputation for doing nothing. He also set his men to digging entrenchments around Richmond. Since he knew McClellan outnumbered him, he wanted to protect his men by using the breastworks as an equalizing influence, allowing him to hold more ground with fewer troops. At this stage of the war, though, his men thought it a cowardly waste of time, and added another insulting nickname to Lee's growing list, calling him the "King of Spades."

Not everyone believed the stories about Lee, though. Joseph Ives had served on Lee's staff briefly, and he had understood Lee better than most. In a discussion on strategy with E. Porter Alexander, who would later serve Lee well as commander of artillery, Alexander asked Ives if Lee was up to the job of command. Ives responded that, "if there is one man in either army, Federal or Confederate, who is . . . far above every other one . . . in audacity that man is Gen. Lee, and you will very soon have lived to see it. Lee is audacity personified."

Chapter 4

LEE ASCENDANT

Even as the men outside Richmond grumbled and complained about "Granny Lee," the "King of Spades," Lee was laying the groundwork for his first significant campaign. His men would soon have more than enough marching and fighting to know that he was anything but slow or timid. Lee had no intention of letting McClellan maintain the initiative, and to him that meant one thing: Attack. Lee had settled this much in his mind early on, but the question then became where and how to do it.

While Lee may have originally been somewhat lukewarm in his enthusiasm for the Confederacy, now his services to it consumed him. It had been more than a year since he had seen Mary, though he wrote to her regularly and saw a good bit of his sons, all by now members of the Confederate army. The attention he had formerly lavished on letters from friends and family now seemed to be strained and, at certain key points, even broken. The best (worst) example of Lee's forgetfulness came while he was planning his grand offensive against McClellan. Rooney and his wife, Charlotte, had earlier become the proud parents of Lee's first grandchild. Sadly, the boy died in infancy and Mary wrote her husband to let him know on June 6, 1862. On June 22, Lee took his pen to inform Charlotte of Rooney's exploits, and ended his letter by asking her to "Kiss your sweet boy for me." Lee was so distracted by the campaign that he had forgotten that his grandson had died.

The "where" part of the attack question was answered by the aggressive and flamboyant antics of Custis's old friend, J.E.B. Stuart. Stuart was now a brigadier general commanding Lee's cavalry. It was his job to control the area around the army, bringing Lee reliable intelligence on what McClellan was doing while preventing McClellan's cavalry from finding out anything about Lee. In mid-June, Stuart asked Lee for discretionary permission to lead a large raid toward the rear of McClellan's army. Lee agreed, hoping to find out if one of the Federal flanks was vulnerable to attack. Stuart left the next day (June 11) with about 1,000 handpicked troopers. He very quickly discovered that McClellan's right was indeed "in the air," a term of military jargon that meant there was nothing that prevented it from being attacked. Though Stuart could have returned immediately, over the next two days he managed to ride around the entire Federal army covering over 100 miles and thoroughly embarrassing the inept Federal cavalry trying to catch him. To make the situation even more ludicrous, Stuart's own father-in-law had led the pursuit. Lucky for Lee, the general outrage over Stuart's daring kept McClellan from realizing what part of his line Lee had actually been scouting. McClellan did nothing to cover his flank.

Since he would strike McClellan's right, the opposite of what Johnston had tried at Seven Pines, Lee wanted to move most of his troops north of the Chickahominy River and launch an overwhelming assault from there. The problem now became how to raise the force he needed without risking Richmond. Lee's army was slightly smaller than McClellan's, even without McDowell in the area, so if he weakened his southern wing too much, then McClellan could punch through it and take the city. Lee's answer was twofold. First, he redoubled his efforts to build up his trenches just east of the city, where the danger would be worst, and he left two smaller divisions there. He expected that the defensive advantages their entrenchments gave them would balance out any excess Federal numbers. Second, he simply knew with confidence that McClellan would not attack. If McClellan were that timid, Lee could risk weakening part of his line. Meanwhile Lee sent word to Jackson to join him from the Shenandoah. The result of all these preparations would come to be known as the Seven Days' Battles.

Though McClellan gave Lee a fright on June 25 with a probing attack on the southern end of his lines, just where the Southerners were weakest, Lee pressed ahead with his plans. Stonewall Jackson was to open the battle on June 26 near Mechanicsville, Virginia, by attacking the exposed flank of McClellan's army with the troops he had brought over from the Shenandoah. Once they heard Jackson's assault begin, troops in front of the Federals led by Ambrose Powell Hill were to attack head on. Lee hoped that, trapped between Jackson and Hill, the Union flank would disintegrate.

The next morning, Lee waited expectantly for news of Jackson's attack, but he heard nothing. Davis later arrived from Richmond to watch the action, but still nothing happened. As Lee's frustration mounted, he finally heard the sound of rifle fire erupt about three o'clock that afternoon, making it clear that the battle was now on. Unfortunately, it was a bloody failure. None of Lee's carefully laid plans had come off as they should. For some reason, probably due to sheer exhaustion, the normally hard-driving Stonewall had not made it to the field in time. In fact, he was still miles away and, worse, had not communicated that fact to Lee. An impatient Hill had launched his own attack anyway. Though they made some local progress, they were soon bloodily repulsed. It cost Lee 1,475 casualties, far more than the Federals lost, and the lines had moved nowhere in particular. Lee retired that night believing he had lost but ready to attack the next day in order to keep the initiative.

When Lee sent his troops forward the next morning to renew the fight, he found that McClellan had done him the favor of turning a tactical defeat into a strategic victory: he had retreated anyway. Though his army was far from beaten, McClellan was whipped mentally and emotionally. He was convinced that Lee outnumbered him and that Lincoln was trying to undercut him. Like Joe Johnston, he would not risk his reputation as the "Little Napoleon" by hazarding a battle he had any chance of losing. Instead, after Mechanicsville, McClellan embarked on a heroic "change of base"—a retreat—away from Richmond to the lower James River. Lee chased McClellan through the Seven Days' Battles of Gaines's Mill (June 27, day three), Savage Station

(June 29, day five), White Oak Swamp/Glendale (June 30, day six) and finally Malvern Hill (July 1, day seven). With one exception, the same basic pattern repeated itself. Lee would organize a textbook attack, but his orders invariably miscarried for some reason, usually due to some inept officer's failure. The Army of Northern Virginia would be repulsed, but McClellan would retreat anyway. The one exception was Gaines's Mill, where Lee did win a tactical victory, but could not capitalize on it. So, while he could claim only one victory, Lee managed to win the campaign and relieved Richmond from the threat of McClellan.

Over the course of the week, Lee learned quite a bit about the difference between planning and execution. Time and again he saw his best intentions disintegrate because his orders simply were not followed. Worse, it was not just the political generals who had failed him, but also a number of West Pointers. Lee continued his policy of transferring men who displeased him away from his army, and a string of officers soon left for parts farther west and south.

This was important to Lee's particular style of command. Lee did not micromanage his battles once they began, preferring to trust his subordinates to take the right steps. "I plan and work with all my might to bring the troops to the right place at the right time," he said later, "with that I have done my duty. As soon as I order the troops forward into battle, I lay the fate of my army in the hands of God." Lee knew that he could not be everywhere at once, and so he trusted his officers to act for him. This approach meshed well with Lee's chronic fear of confrontation. Like a carpenter, Lee preferred to work with the grain of the wood rather than against it. If a person could be made useful, he would work around the knots and deformations. If he found an officer he thought fundamentally flawed, he discarded him.

It is notable that Lee personally continued to set very high standards for himself and his army. He intended to annihilate McClellan's army. With each attack, he wanted to destroy large parts of it, and with each failure his frustrations grew. While historians and pundits have been amazed at what Lee accomplished against McClellan, Lee himself still thought the campaign a failure. Whatever Lee's opinion, the Seven Days began a yearlong run of successes that can be described as nothing short of miraculous.

The Seven Days demonstrate a number of other key themes regarding Lee's generalship beyond his interactions and expectations. Lee was one of the most forward-thinking generals in terms of the tactical and strategic use of entrenchments. To Lee, the shovel was as much a part of military life as the rifle or cannon. All three were to be used in conjunction to magnify the effects of the others. Lee believed wars were won by taking the offensive, but in order to do that, especially in the face of overwhelming odds, he needed soldiers. Fortifications were the great equalizer; they helped him hold key points with the minimum number of men and thereby maximize his attack power. Later in the war, entrenchments became common, and if the troops paused for longer than a few minutes, they would begin building them spontaneously. Lee understood their importance far better than his contemporaries. Another important aspect of Lee's generalship demonstrated during his campaign against McClellan was his uncanny ability to read his opponents. Lee seemed to know precisely what he could and could not get away with. For instance, Lee would try running literal circles around McClellan, John Pope, and Joseph Hooker, but was much more careful when facing George Meade and Grant. He appeared to know intuitively what each person's limits were and how best to exploit them. Finally, Lee was willing to take serious risks in order to reap significant rewards. This ability distinguished him from generals like Johnston and McClellan, who in theory were as able as Lee in terms of tactics and strategy, but never very effective. While they planned well, their fear of failure prevented them from acting decisively. Lee accepted the possibility of failure, but did not let it distract him. He was indeed "audacity personified."

As Lee culled his army for the second time and McClellan cowered against the James, another crisis was brewing to the north. While Lee had been otherwise engaged at Gaines's Mill, Lincoln had been working on creating another army to keep the pressure on the Confederates. Major General John Pope had been successful in the West, and was best known for his victories at New Madrid and Island No. 10. Lincoln now called on him to lead a new force composed of McDowell's corps and those Jackson had so recently humiliated in the Shenandoah Valley, all told approximately 55,000 men. Pope somewhat presumptuously named it the "Army of Virginia."

Pope did not begin his tenure by impressing people inside his army or outside it. One of the first things he did was insult his men in his opening orders. "Let us understand each other," he said. "I have come to you from the West, where we have always seen the backs of our enemies; from an army whose business it has been to seek the adversary and to beat him when he was found; whose policy has been attack and not defense." In that one moment, Pope mocked McClellan (the idol of his troops) and strongly implied that the men of the East were an army of weaklings more worried about running away than they were winning the war. There had already been an unofficial competition going on between the theaters. The Eastern men thought Western soldiers were nothing more than uncouth, uneducated barbarians incapable of an intelligent thought, and the Western men thought the Eastern soldiers little better than overeducated sissies, not man enough for the job. Pope's tenure would do nothing to heal the breech.

Of course, Pope had only just begun insulting the Confederates. He took the first open step toward "hard war" by approaching the South as if it were an enemy rather than a wayward brother. McClellan had been very careful to treat Southerners with kid gloves. He refused to let his men take food, wood, or other supplies from civilians and if any slaves entered his lines seeking freedom, he ordered them returned. McClellan (and at the time, Lincoln) labored under the misconception that most Southerners did not actually support the Confederacy, and that they had been bamboozled by the mythical "slave power conspiracy." If the South could only be convinced that the Union was no threat, then in theory the rebellion could end peacefully. By this time, it had become clear to many people, Lincoln included, that this was not the case. The North would have to get serious about fighting the war if it wanted to win. Pope ordered his men to live off the land, hold civilians accountable for any guerilla attacks, and force all male civilians in the vicinity of the army to take loyalty oaths or be expelled from inside Union lines. Any civilian suspected of hostile acts against his army was liable to be hung. Historian Mark Grimsley has called this the "pragmatic" policy. Pope did not take these steps specifically to hurt Confederate morale. He did it because it helped him fight the war in a more practical way.

The South reacted with indignant howls of complaint. They said that Pope was a criminal who had declared war on innocent women and children. Lee was outraged, declaring Pope a "miscreant" who needed to be "suppressed"—very strong language for Lee. In fact, when compared to warfare from nearly every other period of history before and after it (particularly the Middle Ages and the two World Wars), Pope's measures were quite tame, but the muted atmosphere of the period made them seem worse than they were.

Lee looked forward to the chance to humble Pope, but it was not a simple situation. McClellan still puttered around the James with his army, a significant force if only he chose to use it. Lee had to stay close to McClellan until it became clear that Little Mac did not intend mischief of his own. Lee dispatched Jackson with 12,000 men to face Pope in mid-July while he stayed behind with the rest of the army to watch McClellan. He also wrote forceful letters protesting Pope's policies to Major General Henry Halleck, then in charge of all Union forces. If any civilians were hung, Lee threatened to choose an equal number of captured Federal officers and execute them.

For a short time on August 5, it looked like McClellan did indeed intend to attack Richmond again, catching it in the middle of a north-south pincers movement between himself and Pope. The Army of the Potomac advanced from the James and reoccupied Malvern Hill. Lee moved quickly to meet it, but nothing of importance happened. McClellan stayed on the hill for two days, and then he returned to Harrison's Landing. That convinced Lee that McClellan was not a serious threat, though Pope was. About this time Lee learned that Lincoln was detaching troops from McClellan and sending them to Pope. If this was allowed to continue unhindered, the resulting army would outnumber Jackson by almost 10 to 1 and Lee's entire army substantially.

On August 9, Jackson and Pope clashed at Cedar Mountain. Jackson was much more himself than he had been during the Seven Days, but he still found himself seriously pressed. Though Jackson was able to survive and even call it a victory (it was more of a draw, if anything), Lee knew he would have to send Jackson significant help if he really did want to "suppress" Pope and he must do it soon before McClellan's men reached him.

At first Lee hoped to outmaneuver Pope and press him into a situation where the Federals would have to fight on Lee's terms. Unfortunately, the normally competent J.E.B. Stuart had a bad day and was nearly captured by Union cavalry. While Stuart escaped, an order outlining Lee's plan of attack did not. A series of other blunders and failures meant that Pope knew what Lee intended to do and was able to pull his troops out of the way in time. Stuart later returned the favor by slipping behind Federal lines and nearly capturing Pope. He managed to come back with Pope's dispatch case, which confirmed what Lee had already known about Pope's plans.

Lee caught up with Jackson on August 24 and discussed his next plan with him. Lee had no intention of giving up the initiative, and, as usual, his intentions were bold. Lee proposed to send Jackson on a massive raid with 23,000 men around Pope's flank and into his rear. Lee would wait with the commander of his other wing, James Longstreet, for Jackson to cause trouble, and then they would join him to finish Pope. The plan was daring, perhaps dangerously so, but it would also be unexpected. One of the most basic rules of warfare at the time was that a general should never divide his forces, especially in the face of a superior enemy. Lee seems to have crossed this idea out of his manual of war, as he repeatedly violated it. Dividing his forces invited disaster by making it possible for the army to be "destroyed in detail." This meant that since each part of the force would be seriously inferior to the enemy, the enemy could attack each piece and destroy it easily. In this case, if Pope realized what was happening, he could attack either Jackson or Longstreet with his entire army. If he could catch one of them alone, he would almost certainly destroy half of Lee's army.

Jackson, excited to pursue his own brand of war once again, left on August 25. He moved undetected around Pope's flank and into the rear of his army. At Bristoe Station Jackson paused to derail a few of the supply trains heading for Pope's army, his men cheering while they watched the massive crashes. This alerted Pope to Jackson's move, but Pope could not find him. On August 27, Jackson hit Pope's main supply depot at Manassas Junction. There his men found tons of supplies the cash-strapped Confederacy had been forced to ration—food (the lobster salad was a favorite), clothing, ammunition, and, of course, "medicinal" whiskey. Jackson let his troops gorge themselves and carry off as much as they could. He then set fire to the remnants, destroying them and escaping cleanly. A frustrated Pope entered town soon afterward to find nothing but the smoldering remains of his bacon and hardtack. The next day, Jackson fell back to a position on the old Bull Run battlefield and waited for Pope to catch up with him.

Meanwhile, Lee tried to follow Jackson. Longstreet ran into some resistance around Thoroughfare Gap that forced him to deploy his troops and fight his way through. This slowed his progress significantly and meant that Pope had a chance to make Lee's nightmare of defeat in detail become reality. If the guns in the gap could hold out longer than Jackson, the Army of Northern Virginia might soon cease to exist. Rather than wait for Longstreet, Jackson launched an attack of his own. On August 28, he fought an indecisive action that still had its intended effect, which was to distract Pope's attention away from Lee and allow the rest of the Rebel army to get into place. Pope fell for the ruse and focused all of his attention on Jackson, whom he was convinced was retreating in disorder.

The next day Pope advanced on Jackson's army and pressed hard. Jackson had taken a position along an unfinished railroad that provided his men with some cover. Pope intended to hit Jackson on both flanks, while holding him in the center. His orders miscarried, though, and the attacks went in one at a time, giving Jackson the chance to beat each one off. Had all the attacks gone in as Pope intended, Jackson would probably have broken, but he managed to hold on, even though his troops had to resort to throwing stones when they ran out of ammunition.

While Jackson fought for his life, Longstreet filed his men into place on Pope's flank. Jackson and Pope had been facing each other in lines more or less parallel. Longstreet lined his men up on Pope's flank, making the Confederate line look like a huge "L" with a bend greater than 90 degrees. This left Pope's army hovering between the arms. While Jackson fought, Lee sent several communications forward to Longstreet suggesting that he attack. Lee was worried not only for Jackson, but that Pope would discover their presence and would retreat out of the trap when he realized his peril. Longstreet refused three times, and Lee deferred to his judgment.

James Longstreet was an interesting man. Born in South Carolina in 1821, he had been a career army officer when he resigned to go south in 1861. He had earned a promotion to major general for his actions at First Bull Run, but had caused trouble for Johnston at Seven Pines/Fair Oaks by throwing off the Confederate attack plan significantly when he refused to yield a road. Longstreet had performed well under Lee in the Seven Days, though, and so had not been sent away as others had been. Longstreet was a very opinionated man who believed that he was a superior commander to Lee. He quickly established a habit of questioning Lee's orders and even changing them, if he thought it necessary. Given Lee's distaste for confrontation, he would sometimes let Longstreet get away with more than he should have. It is notable, though, that Lee rarely trusted Longstreet with the kinds of independent commands he gave to Jackson. Still, Longstreet quickly joined Jackson as one of Lee's most experienced and competent commanders, leading Lee to call him "my old warhorse."

The next morning, August 30, Lee worried that they had missed their chance. He need not have. Pope was still oblivious to Longstreet's presence, and instead assumed that the movement he saw around him indicated Jackson beating a hasty retreat in the hopes of saving his army. At about 1 P.M., Pope sent virtually his entire force forward in "pursuit." He found Jackson still in place and before he could recover from his blunder, Longstreet crushed his flank completely. Pope's army fell away from the field in confusion but recovered quickly enough to prevent a total rout. Lee tried to press Pope, but Pope's own handling of the retreat, the sheer exhaustion of Lee's men, and a post-battle rainstorm combined to prevent an effective pursuit. Pope's demoralized and frightened army was able to make it back into the defenses of Washington.

The next day, as Lee was still trying to find a way to maintain the initiative, something spooked Traveller and he reared. Lee, standing on the ground next to him, instinctively reached for the reins. Traveller yanked Lee off balance and the general fell face forward. Lee tried to catch himself with his hands, but sprained both of his wrists badly and broke a small bone. Doctors had him cleaned up and in splints quickly, but Lee would not be able to write, ride, or dress himself without help for weeks to come. He would follow his army in an ambulance.

When it became clear that he would not catch Pope, Lee turned his attention to a grander campaign. He knew he wanted to maintain the pressure on the North and perhaps win another dramatic battle, this time on Northern soil. Through dictation, he proposed to Jefferson Davis that he invade Maryland and see what trouble he could cause for Lincoln there. Lee argued that such an expedition might result in recruits for his army (as Maryland slaveholders deserted the Union for the Confederacy) and that it would give Virginia an opportunity to recuperate from the fighting of the past year. Davis was unsure of this idea, but let Lee proceed with a limited invasion.

The discussion over Lee's plans demonstrated the different philosophies of war espoused by Lee and Davis. Davis had always expected to win his war much like Washington had won the Revolution: Through attrition and willpower. Davis intended to organize a wholly defensive conflict and simply keep fighting until the Union got tired of it and agreed to peace. In order to do that, Davis wanted to spread Confederate forces thin and try to avoid major losses, accepting the smaller ones he thought inevitable. Lee saw things differently. He knew that the Union had just as great an advantage over the Confederacy as the British had over their colonies in terms of industry, technology, finances, and manpower. Unlike Britain, however, the Union was not separated from the Confederacy by an ocean. This made Lee believe that they could not hope to outlast the Union. Lee therefore favored forcing a decision through one or two grand victories that would so demoralize the North that they would choose to give up. If Lee's plan were followed, the Confederacy would pull all its forces together into one massive army and gamble it all on an invasion exactly like the one Lee was pursuing.

As historian Steven E. Woodworth has observed, these were both viable plans, but they were obviously also mutually exclusive propositions. Lee, of course, could not contradict Davis and declare his policy if the president was set on another. He did not simply accept Davis's approach, however. Lee was able to push his plans forward, as he did here, by working with Davis rather than against him. Given Davis's personality, this was a very tricky thing for anyone and most of the other Confederate generals, including Johnston and Beauregard, failed at it miserably. Davis was an intelligent, hard working individual with as much experience in military matters as some of his commanders, but he was also sensitive and prickly. He took his role as commander in chief very seriously, and would meddle with his armies far more often than Lincoln did with his. The fact that Davis was also regularly ill during the war and refused to relinquish his duties only made things worse. Lee was one of the few men who knew how to handle the president. He was able to adopt the right tone of deference and seemed to know precisely how hard and how far to push Davis.

The result did not work well for the Confederacy. Davis would give way to Lee, but Lee could never convince him to completely abandon the attrition strategy. As a result, they met somewhere in the middle and neither plan was implemented fully. Davis never released enough troops for Lee to win his knockout victory, but Lee sapped more than enough troops away from Davis to prevent his holding the territory he needed to hold. Worse, when Lee lost the occasional gamble, it resulted in the sort of embarrassing failure Davis wanted to avoid.

Once again, Lee's plans were dramatic, more so, in fact, than he had actually shared with Davis. When the army got moving on September 5, Lee started a series of letters to Davis, keeping him fully informed of what he was about, but sent at intervals that meant Davis would never receive them in time to contradict Lee's plans. Now, rather than engage in a limited campaign in Maryland, Lee intended to advance into Pennsylvania. He tried to move as swiftly as he could, hoping to take advantage of the presumed demoralization of Union forces. He again split his army in the face of the enemy. One half (under Jackson) advanced directly west to the Shenandoah Valley where it was to take Harpers Ferry, located at the head of the valley. Lee and Longstreet would meet Jackson there and use the valley as a protected supply line. They would then try to force the decisive battle of the war.

This time Lee failed to fully anticipate George McClellan's luck. While Lincoln had hoped to be rid of him after Second Bull Run, with Lee's invasion imminent, Lincoln had to turn somewhere quickly. There was no time to call another commander from the west, and if McClellan had proved himself capable of one thing, it was rebuilding a demoralized army. McClellan went to work with spirit and managed a nearly miraculous transformation in the battered and beaten Army of the Potomac. While it would take time to fully repair morale, in a matter of days McClellan turned his men into a viable fighting force once again.

Lee still was not worried as his army passed through Frederick, Maryland on its way to the mountains. He knew McClellan. Even if "Little Mac" had managed to pull everyone together, he would still come on slowly. By the time McClellan got moving, Lee planned to be far ahead. While camped outside of Frederick on the night of September 9, Lee ordered several copies of Special Orders No. 191, containing the complete plan of campaign, distributed to his division commanders. The next morning the army moved on.

McClellan followed Lee at his usual speed. By sheer coincidence, Union soldiers camped on some of the same ground outside Frederick that Lee's men had occupied. Several troops noticed a small package lying next to a fencepost. It contained three cigars wrapped in a document: Special Orders No. 191. It took a little while for the men to realize the importance of what they had found and then for it to work its way up the chain of command, but by September 13 McClellan had read, in detail, Lee's entire plan of campaign. As "Little Mac" put it, "Here is a paper with which if I cannot whip Bobby Lee I will be willing to go home." He knew Lee's strength and where he was headed. McClellan began to move his army with resolute speed, at least for him. Where another commander might have destroyed Lee outright, McClellan still moved slowly enough that Lee was able to react.

Lee was initially surprised by McClellan's actions. If McClellan caught him before he could reassemble his army, "Little Mac" was virtually guaranteed to annihilate the Army of Northern Virginia. Worse, many of Lee's men, horses, and mules had not fully recovered from the earlier campaign and had begun to straggle behind the army, reducing his army by roughly one-third of its original number. When he heard that McClellan had copies of his plan, Lee immediately sent orders to concentrate for battle.

Lee needed to pull his forces together, but doing it would not be easy. McClellan was now approaching fast behind the part of his force that was in Maryland, and Jackson had not yet had the opportunity to take Harpers Ferry. The Federals had a substantial garrison there that Lee would need to eliminate if he hoped to survive. Lee sent orders to Jackson to take the city as quickly as possible, while he held the key passes through South Mountain with some of Longstreet's men. The vanguard of McClellan's army took the passes on September 14, but did not immediately advance, giving Lee the needed breathing room.

On the morning of September 15 the Federal commander at Harpers Ferry surrendered and Lee decided to make a stand. He ordered Jackson to send as many men as he could spare to Sharpsburg, Maryland and then follow with the rest as soon as possible. Lee laid out his line along a series of hills outside of town. To his rear, there was only a single ford across the Potomac River. If his army broke, he would be virtually guaranteed to lose everything. The southern end of his line followed Antietam Creek, though the northern end bent back around Sharpsburg and away from the creek. Per their respective customs, the South named the upcoming battle for the closest city while the North named it for the closest body of water.

McClellan arrived on the field opposite Lee on September 16, but did not attack. His continued delay gave Lee the chance to bring in more reinforcements from Harpers Ferry, and Lee needed every man he could get. Though many of Jackson's men had arrived, Lee was still missing A.P. Hill's large division, leaving him with just under 40,000 men to face McClellan's army of over 70,000. As usual, McClellan greatly overestimated Lee's numbers, and he sent a stream of whining telegrams back to Washington highlighting the care he was taking in light of the impossible odds he supposedly faced. All the while, McClellan outnumbered Lee by an almost two to one margin.

The battle opened on September 17, 1862, on what was to become the bloodiest single day in American history, only rivaled at this time by the September 11, 2001 attacks on the World Trade Center and Washington, D.C. McClellan ordered three attacks on Lee's line, but thanks to almost nonexistent coordination, they went in one at a time. Lee was able to shift troops from one place to another, hanging on by the slimmest of margins.

The first major assault came on Lee's northern flank. Union major generals Joseph J. Hooker and Joseph Mansfield (who had worked with Lee on Cockspur Island) thrust through a cornfield and penetrated the Confederate line. Lee moved troops from the southern end of the field and Jackson was able to stabilize that front, but only just. The fire was so heavy that it cut through men and corn alike, felling them all into bloody rows on the ground. Each side so shredded the other that the men in that area were unable to contribute to the fighting for the rest of the battle.

The second assault started about midday, near the time that the first had ground to a halt. This time, the Federals attacked a portion of the line that came to be known as the "Bloody Lane," near the middle of Lee's line. At first the Confederates held off their attackers from behind cover, but soon a bungled order left them exposed and a Union assault decimated them. Again, Lee's line had been cracked wide open. Again, the Army of the Potomac failed to capitalize on its advantage and Lee was just able to plug the hole.

The final part of the battle started about three o'clock that afternoon. Thousands of Union troops under Major General Ambrose Burnside tried charging a bridge over the Antietam (later called "Burnside's Bridge") held by about 500 Georgia soldiers. The Georgians used the bridge as a bottleneck, forcing the much larger Federal forces into a tight space where they could be mowed down. Finally, after repeated charges, the Confederates began to run low on ammunition and were flanked out of their position when Burnside's men found other ways across the Antietam. Burnside soon had his entire corps across and shattered Lee's line. This time, Lee had no more troops to shift. It appeared that the end had come.

Even in the face of the total destruction of his army, Lee did not lose his composure. In the distance to the south, he could make out a cloud of dust moving up a road. He asked a nearby soldier to use his spyglass to identify whose troops they were. The man offered the eyepiece to Lee, who held up his still bandaged hands in answer. The soldier looked out at the dust and reported, "They are flying the Virginia and Confederate flags." Lee showed no visible signs of emotion, but quietly replied, "It is A.P. Hill from Harper's Ferry." It was indeed Hill, bringing with him his Light Division, the very last troops in Lee's army. Lee ordered them forward, and they made a desperate screaming charge that bottled up Burnside's troops, sealing the final breach of the day.

Lee remained in place the next day, daring McClellan to attack him. Many of his stragglers had come up during the night, restoring his numbers somewhat, and Lee thought that the troop's morale had improved enough that he could resist another assault. McClellan was more than able to follow through, but once again let the opportunity pass. The

Army of the Potomac had entire divisions that had not seen any action. Had they pressed Lee there was a strong chance of success, but silence reigned on the field except for the cries of the wounded and dying. Unable to resume the offensive, Lee retreated back across the Potomac into friendly territory on September 19. McClellan followed impotently, as usual.

The Antietam Campaign was over, and the country had paid a fearful price. Lee's army of 40,000 had suffered 10,000 casualties, while he had caused 12,000 in McClellan's. Of these, nearly 4,000 were dead. Lee had lost almost one quarter of his army, but they had managed to survive to continue the war. Rather than simply giving the army strategic direction, Lee had been forced to take a much more personal hand in this battle. He had been present on each part of the front at the critical moment, and had directed his men personally. Lee had gambled and this time he had nearly lost. Had his opponent been other than McClellan, he almost certainly would have.

As Lee returned to Virginia to rest, refit, and joust with the ever tentative Army of the Potomac, the Confederates suffered more reverses.

The Confederate dead at Antietam. (Library of Congress.)

The most obvious of these came with the retreat of one of its main western armies back into Tennessee. Thinking that the citizens of the slave state of Kentucky would surely rally to the flag of the Confederacy, Major General Braxton Bragg had led the Army of Tennessee on a mission of "liberation" into the Blue Grass State, much like Lee had Maryland. There, he found that most Kentuckians were not interested in leaving the Union. In fact, almost all of those inclined to join the Confederate Army had already done so. After some inconclusive sparring with Union general Don Carlos Buell that October, Bragg retreated.

Of more lasting importance, Lincoln had taken the opportunity offered by Lee's retreat to issue his Emancipation Proclamation. In it, he declared any and all slaves in areas still in rebellion against the United States as of January 1, 1863 would be forever free. While some historians have noted that in effect Lincoln was freeing only those slaves he had no power to free, Lincoln's foresight has outshone their hindsight. While virtually no slaves walked free that New Year's Day, millions would over the course of the next few years. More important for present purposes, Lincoln changed the nature of the war. Up to this point, while the evil of slavery lurked beneath the ultimate causes of the war, both sides had studiously avoided admitting it. Its emotional guilt over slavery aside, the South knew that most of the foreign countries they hoped to recruit to their cause would not support a revolution for slavery. In the North, many people willing to risk life and limb to defend the Union would not be willing to do the same to free the slaves. Also, in the early part of the war, Lincoln had hoped to conciliate the South into ending the fighting, and so wanted to show them he was no threat to their way of life. With the Emancipation Proclamation, everything was out in the open and Lincoln had declared that the Union could never be restored to what it had been before the war. The British in particular recoiled from helping the Confederacy, and the French would not act without them. Both North and South prepared to face a longer, harder fight. Lee does not seem to have made any particular response to the Emancipation Proclamation. He simply accepted it and its effect on the war and moved on to the next stage of the fighting.

Lincoln had other matters to attend to as well. In particular, he was through dealing with McClellan and he used his poor performance in the Antietam Campaign to send him packing permanently. In his place, Lincoln turned to a man who felt completely unqualified for the job: Ambrose Burnside. Burnside tried to dissuade Lincoln from making the choice, but to no avail. He took command of the Army of the Potomac from his friend McClellan and prepared for operations of his own. When Lee heard the news, he was understandably disappointed. "[We] always understood each other so well," he said of McClellan. "I fear they may continue to make these changes till they find some one whom I don't understand."

Chapter 5

THE HIGH ROAD TO GETTYSBURG

Ambrose Burnside was a genuinely likeable man. He was also reasonably intelligent, having invented his own breech loading carbine rifle. He might be best known for the hair on his face. People have since inverted the name but kept the style he created: the sideburn. Now 38 years old, he had a West Point education and had worked for McClellan before the war, later becoming one of Little Mac's corps commanders. If he had displayed a weakness as a commander thus far, it was revealed in one of his strengths: Burnside was steady and strong, not easily diverted from his goals. While normally not bad, this left Burnside unable to adapt to new situations quickly, as shown in his dogged determination to get across the bridge that bore his name at Antietam, even as his men were slaughtered by the defenders. This was the man that Lee now faced across the Rappahannock River, as intent as his predecessors on taking the Confederate capital and destroying the Army of Northern Virginia.

Burnside had seen some worthy successes along the North Carolina coast earlier in the war, and that had brought him to the attention of Lincoln in his search for a general to replace McClellan. When Lincoln approached him about it, Burnside tried to refuse command. Unlike other generals who sometimes put on a show of humility, Burnside truly believed that he could not do the job. Lincoln pressed him, however, and Burnside nervously agreed.

Meanwhile, Lee stayed focused on the war, even as his family faced significant personal losses. When Lee agreed to take command of the army, he went in wholeheartedly. He did not split his attention, even to visit his family. He corresponded with them regularly and saw his sons in the service, but he took no time off to return to Mary or his daughters, who by now were scattered over Virginia after the loss of Arlington to the Federals. Every morning, when he opened his mail, he read his professional messages first and only then turned to anything personal. Lee's assistant Taylor was working with him one morning in the fall of 1862 and had already run several errands for him. He returned to Lee's tent and found him "overcome with grief, an open letter in his hands." Lee's daughter Annie, a favorite, had died of typhoid fever on October 20 at the age of 23. Lee mastered himself and went back to work, but the loss of his daughter haunted him. "In the quiet hours of the night," he later said, "when there is nothing to lighten the full weight of my grief, I feel as if I should be overwhelmed."

One continuing frustration for the Lincoln administration had been that for some reason, its commanders never seemed able to bring all of their overwhelming forces to bear against Lee at once. That was precisely the problem that Burnside intended to rectify in his new plan. The Army of the Potomac would march quickly to Fredericksburg, Virginia, where they would cross the Rappahannock River and advance toward Richmond. This should draw Lee out of the mountains and into the open as he attempted to defend the capital. When that happened, Burnside would overwhelm Lee with sheer offensive firepower. The plan was solid, if unimaginative, just as Burnside himself was. The problem was making it happen in real life.

The first stages of the plan worked beautifully. Burnside began his march toward Fredericksburg on November 15 and his men began arriving on November 17. Lee reacted by sending a small force, but he did not move decisively, as he was not convinced that Fredericksburg really was Burnside's ultimate goal. There were a number of other options for Burnside to try, but he chose one of the most direct. Even when it became apparent that the whole army was headed to Fredericksburg,

Lee delayed his march, giving the Federals an opportunity to cross the river before the Army of Northern Virginia could get there in significant force to oppose them.

Had Burnside managed to press on immediately, his plan stood a chance of working. Unfortunately, the Union army had forgotten a key piece of equipment: their pontoon bridges. These were essentially boats that the armies could string together side by side from one bank of a river to the other and then lay planks across to form a serviceable bridge when and where they needed it. Though Burnside had ordered the bridges to Fredericksburg, a mix up in the War Department had sent them elsewhere. Without his pontoons, Burnside could not cross the river, and if he could not cross the river in a timely manner, then the campaign would in all likelihood end in failure. Lee would get to Fredericksburg and contest the crossing.

Still, Burnside had also observed McClellan's example: McClellan's slowness and lack of potent initiative had destroyed his career. That lesson went hand in hand with Burnside's own stubborn personality to produce an effect for which Lee could hardly have hoped: If the bridges were not there, then Burnside would wait for them, even if it took weeks. He would not end his campaign or alter his plans. He would rely on determination and the sheer power of his army. That decision gave Lee almost leisure time to prepare what would become one of the best defensive positions history has known since the one the Spartans had enjoyed at Thermopylae.

Lee reached Fredericksburg on November 20 and helped its citizens evacuate the dangerous territory between the two armies. The town was situated next to the river, and ridges rose up on both sides. On the northern side, on Stafford Heights, Burnside had arrayed the impressive collection of Federal artillery with which he bombarded the town. On the southern side, an open field led from the town up to Marye's Heights, a long ridge that roughly paralleled the river. There was a drainage ditch that could only be easily crossed with a few small bridges close to the Fredericksburg side of the field. Right below the heights, a road ran, worn deeper by years of wagon travel, and between the road and the field stood a sturdy stone wall.

Lee ordered his artillery to occupy Marye's Heights and placed Longstreet's men directly under them, in the lane behind the wall. They had a clear, open field of fire that swept almost all of the plain below. It was so well suited to defensive artillery that when Lee asked his commander, Edward Porter Alexander, what he thought of it, Alexander replied that when his guns opened, "a chicken could not live on that field." Lee then placed Jackson's troops in a line leading out from Longstreet's right. Jackson also occupied a ridge overlooking the flood plain, but because of the lay of the land, his position was much weaker than the nearly impenetrable front along the lane. In fact, several commanders were worried that Longstreet's position was so strong that Burnside would not dare attack it.

On the night of December 10, Burnside began building his pontoon bridges for the assault. At daylight on December 11, Confederates concealed in the ruins of Fredericksburg opened fire, killing so many of the workers that the rest had to retreat. Union artillery attacked the town again but could not drive off the snipers. Finally, groups of soldiers used the pontoons as assault boats to cross the river and chase the Confederates off. A nasty street battle erupted, but eventually the last of Lee's men retreated back to their lines. That night, a frustrated Army of the Potomac vandalized the town, angering Lee.

When the sun rose on the bitter, cold morning of December 13, the southern shore of the Rappahannock swarmed with blue Federals. According to Burnside's plans, their largest and heaviest blow would fall directly on the Marye's Heights position, while a smaller attack would press Jackson. This was, of course, precisely what Lee wanted. As the Army of the Potomac advanced, they would bunch up at the bridges over the drainage ditch outside of town, which happened to lie in range of Longstreet's men. Then they had to charge across yards of open ground under heavy fire from the Confederates behind the wall (which formed a perfect entrenchment for the Confederate infantry) while being pummeled by the artillery massed on Marye's Heights.

Despite Burnside's best efforts, it quickly degenerated into a brutal slaughter. Wave after wave of men came charging across the field, only to be shot down before they reached the wall. With so many men being thrown at him, Lee worried that Longstreet's lines might break, but Longstreet replied confidently that "if you put every man now on the other side of the Potomac on that field to approach me over the same line, and give me plenty of ammunition, I will kill them all before they reach my line." True to his word, not a single Union soldier reached the wall that day. The survivors simply lay down where they were, using the bodies of their fallen comrades as makeshift shields to protect them from the storm of lead bursting all around.

The real danger for Lee came on Jackson's front, when Major General George Meade found a hole in the Confederate lines and punched through. In a series of hard fought, desperate skirmishes, Jackson managed to seal the breach and hold on, though it cost him several thousand casualties. Lee kept his attention focused on the attacks against Longstreet, however. As he watched the men falling by the dozens before his guns, he remarked, "It is well that war is so terrible—we should grow too fond of it!"

Lee's generals urged him to counterattack Burnside the next day, but he refused. He believed that, even after the pure murder of the 13th, Burnside would attack him again. Though the idea may sound insane, Lee actually understood Burnside quite well. After the slaughter, a guilt-ridden Burnside was filled with grand ideas about last charges and fighting to the death rather than facing the dishonor of living with such an ignoble defeat on his conscience. Only the intervention of his generals prevented him from ordering another charge against Marye's Heights the next day, which he planned to personally lead. During the night of December 14–15, the Army of the Potomac withdrew back across the river to safety.

The Battle of Fredericksburg was over, and it had resulted in one of the most lopsided victories of Lee's career. Burnside had suffered 12,653 casualties to Lee's 5,377. It was an amazing accomplishment, due as much to Burnside's pigheaded determination as to Lee's skill. Still, Lee saw the specter of ultimate defeat in even this great victory. If the Union remained dedicated to the war, the Confederacy would lose, even if he won another dozen battles like Fredericksburg. The United States could absorb those losses, while the Confederacy could not.

Lee spent Christmas 1862 away from his family, though he corresponded with them often. He also had to attend to the last provisions of his father-in-law's will. On December 29, he sent notice that the slaves at the various plantations he had inherited control of from

George Washington Parke Custis should be emancipated. They could stay or leave as they liked, but if they agreed to stay they must continue to work as usual, though for pay. The money they earned would be set aside for them for when they decided to go. Lee hired his personal servant and cook and paid them in cash to keep working with him. He hoped that they would start saving money for their future immediately. So, ironically, Lee freed his slaves two days before Lincoln would have thanks to his Emancipation Proclamation.

Of course Lee's action must be put into perspective. Many of the slaves he had ordered emancipated were already freed by the occupying Federal army in places like Arlington or the White House. He was in fact several months overdue to release his slaves, and then was concerned about the effects emancipation would have on the good order and functioning at the plantations. In the end, though, Lee did choose his conscience over his desire for the status quo, and that is something of note, especially with so much else to occupy his mind.

As 1863 dawned, much had changed for Lee and for the Confederacy. Lee had become a full general in command of what was rapidly becoming an army of legend. He had won some of the most amazing battles in United States history, fighting against the very same government he had served so faithfully for so long. He had also become famous. In the early months of the war, the Confederate press had cast about looking for a hero to promote. It had tried Beauregard, Johnston, and Jackson, but it finally settled on Lee (who had to share the spotlight with Jackson for a time). Admirers from all over the Confederacy sent him gifts of food and clothing, which he normally ordered distributed to his men.

Another change had come over his men. They no longer regarded him as "Granny Lee" or "The King of Spades." His men loved him and trusted him like no other. Johnston still cherished false hopes of taking command back from Lee when he had recovered, but this was simply moonshine. The Army of Northern Virginia belonged to Robert E. Lee as long as he could command it. It would fight and die at his order. Lee believed that if he and his men could just remain undefeated for another year and perhaps win a startling victory on Northern soil, public opinion in the North would sour and the Republicans would lose power. If so, the Confederacy could then win by negotiation.

In the middle of January, Burnside tried to renew the campaign against Lee, but failed miserably, though this time Lee had nothing to do with it. That winter proved to be one of the coldest and wettest of recent years, alternating between deluges of rain and bitter cold. About the time Burnside began his movement, so did a rainstorm of Biblical proportions. The Army of the Potomac sank into the mud, covering only a few miles a day. Mules and horses mired up to their knees had to be shot when they broke their legs, and they had sunk so deep in mud their carcasses remained standing. Cannon had to be abandoned until the following spring when the soldiers could return and dig them out. The helpful Confederate soldiers on the far side of river held up signs pointing the way to Richmond.

The "Mud March," as it came to be called, saw the end of Burnside's command. One of the more ambitious of his corps commanders, Major General Joseph J. Hooker, led a successful movement to have him ousted. In Burnside's place, Lincoln appointed Hooker himself. Hooker set about reorganizing and re-equipping the Army of the Potomac. He exuded self-confidence and promised a hard-hitting, intelligent campaign that he was sure would destroy Lee. "May God have mercy on Bobby Lee," he said, "for I shall have none."

Hooker was another West Point graduate who had served with distinction in the old army, particularly in Mexico. Lee probably remembered him best for testifying against Winfield Scott and for Pillow in the pointless court martial after the war. Hooker had also tried to make a living as a civilian, but had failed to the point that he had to borrow money to move back east to volunteer in the present conflict. He had served well as a division and corps commander, earning the nickname "Fighting Joe" from a popular newspaper misprint during the Seven Days. On a personal level, Hooker was a shifty politician, drunkard, and womanizer who alienated as many people as he wooed. His headquarters earned a reputation as the sort of place "no gentleman cared to go, and no lady could go."

Hooker accomplished another miracle cure for the Army of the Potomac, which was proving quite resilient, if nothing else. In a matter of only a few months, he took a demoralized mass of men, most absent from duty without leave, and turned them into a trim fighting force once again. His ranks swelled to more than 120,000. Hooker's confidence

Robert E. Lee during the war. (Library of Congress.)

was infectious, and very soon almost everyone believed that with Hooker as their leader they would simply march south and crush "Bobby" Lee once and for all.

Meanwhile, Lee continued working with his own army, but he faced a new problem that spring: personal illness. His health had not yet begun to suffer seriously, but as time wore on, he himself called it "indifferent." Given his talent for downplaying his own troubles through understatement, it is quite possible that the rough life he was living had begun to tell on him. In his letters to friends and family, he had already reported troubles with his joints and mentioned how little rest he was getting. In late March 1863, he fell seriously ill. He had been fighting a cold for some time before being bedridden by what he called "some malady which must be dreadful if it resembled its name. . . ." He suffered from uncontrollable coughing and sharp chest pains that were probably a re-emergence of the *angina pectoris* he had experienced previously. Though he improved rapidly when allowed to resume his routine, he never fully recovered. For now he wrote off any problems to "old age & sorrow" and moved on.

With the upcoming campaign preparing to get under way, Hooker intended to use his overwhelming numbers to trap Lee. Hooker would leave 25,000 of his men at Fredericksburg under John Sedgwick and then personally march west with the other 75,000. There, he hoped to find undefended routes across the Rappahannock and Rapidan Rivers that would let him arrive on Lee's flank and draw him out of his position at Fredericksburg. In the meantime, Hooker's cavalry, 10,000 strong, would raid Lee's lines of communication with Richmond. In theory, it should be the perfect opportunity to trap Lee. If Lee turned and attacked Hooker, Sedgwick could cross the river and attack Lee's rear. If Lee stayed in Fredericksburg, Hooker would hit his flank. If Lee retired after the cavalry, it could hold out until the entire army arrived and destroyed Lee.

Hooker's advantage was even greater than he realized. Lee had used the lull in February to dispatch Longstreet to southeastern Virginia where he was to counter Federal plans in the area and gather supplies for the army. Once there, Longstreet had besieged Lee with ideas about how he could really serve the war effort better down there (in independent command) than back with the Army of Northern Virginia. Rather than confront Longstreet, Lee bowed to his discretion repeatedly. Two unfortunate side effects resulted from Lee's decision. First and most immediately, Longstreet was absent for the entire Battle of Chancellorsville, which left Lee outnumbered by a margin of two to one. Second, Longstreet began to believe that he was really the intelligent commander in the army and that Lee should and would follow his suggestions.

When Hooker finally began moving in earnest on April 29, Lee could see what he was doing but was unsure how to react to it. He told Davis via telegram that, "their intention, I presume, is to turn our left & probably get into our rear." Earlier in the same note he lamented that "I have nothing to oppose all that force up there." By that evening, though, Lee started to move. He left Jubal Early in command of a small screening force in the Marye's Heights position outside Fredericksburg and marched west to face Hooker.

Had Hooker followed through on all his offensive bluster, then in fact there would have been very little Lee could have done. But Lee found in Hooker another compliant general in charge of the Army of the Potomac. Whereas Hooker's original plan had called for him to charge straight into Lee's flank, once he crossed the rivers he chose to sit down in an area known as the Wilderness at a place called Chancellorsville and wait for Lee. The Wilderness was a dense area of tangled undergrowth where it was difficult to find well-made trails and almost impossible to see farther than a few yards away. This completely nullified Hooker's considerable advantage in artillery, since the crews servicing the guns had to be able to see their target in order to hit it. Also, since Hooker had ordered all of his cavalry away on the raid, he had no practical way of tracking Lee's movements or covering up his own intentions. This went a significant way toward minimizing the long odds Lee faced.

Next, Hooker inexplicably switched from the offensive to the defensive. On May 1, the armies met in earnest. Hooker started to press Lee and then suddenly changed his mind. Not long after the fight had begun, he ordered his men to retreat to their original positions around Chancellorsville and wait. Over the course of the day, he sent contradictory orders to his troops on whether he intended to attack or defend, particularly confusing Oliver O. Howard, in command of the Eleventh Corps on his right flank, and Sedgwick in Fredericksburg. As a result Howard did not take the proper care to secure the end of his line, thinking it protected by the thickness of the Wilderness at that point and that he would resume the march soon anyway. Sedgwick, unsure of what Hooker wanted him to do, sat still in Fredericksburg rather than crossing the river and attacking. Hooker's plan was unraveling, and most of it was his own doing.

Lee, of course, was glad to do what he could to help it unravel even faster. That evening he met with Jackson and planned the next day's battle. Stuart had discovered that Howard had left the end of his line vulnerable to attack, and some local soldiers had offered to guide Jackson to the area. Jackson proposed to take his entire corps and march around Hooker's army. He would then attack Howard's flank, and if he succeeded, he would be in a position to punish if not outright destroy the Army of the Potomac. When Lee asked what forces Jackson intended to leave behind, Jackson replied that he would leave two divisions. Lee agreed and Jackson left to make preparations.

Once again, Lee demonstrated his willingness to ignore the "rules" of warfare if he understood his opponent well and thought the possible rewards great enough. Hooker outnumbered him two to one. Lee had split his army once already, leaving Early in Fredericksburg with 10,000 to face 25,000. Now, Lee had dispatched Jackson with 26,000 of his remaining 43,000 men, leaving Lee with only 17,000 men to keep 75,000 Union troops in check. It would seem that Lee's audacity knew no bounds.

Jackson got moving early in the morning of May 2, but his march covered a serpentine 14-mile route that at times brought him dangerously close to Hooker's lines. If Hooker caught on to what was happening, he would order a general attack and the results would be disastrous for Lee. Lee had the men who remained behind make loud demonstrations to keep Hooker occupied. Far from thinking that he was about to be attacked, Hooker interpreted what was happening as evidence of a Confederate retreat. Finally, late that afternoon, Jackson attacked Howard's men as they settled down to what they thought would be a quiet dinner. He completely crushed Hooker's flank, while Lee attacked from the front. Though the Federal army showed some signs of stabilizing the front, only darkness prevented the attack from being even more successful.

That night Lee was awakened by a messenger bearing terrible news: Jackson had been struck down at the very pinnacle of his success. "Stonewall" had ridden forward to reconnoiter the position of Union troops himself and his group had been mistaken for a Union cavalry patrol when it returned. The jumpy Confederate sentries had shot at them, sparking a rolling wave of firing down the line. Jackson had been hit and was right then undergoing surgery to amputate his left arm. Command of Jackson's wing had devolved to Stuart, who was leading infantry for the first time in his life. Lee sent Jackson his sympathies, but focused his attention on how to best strike Hooker the next day. He ordered Stuart to press ahead and try to cut the Army of the Potomac off from its line of retreat.

At dawn on May 3, Stuart and Lee attacked again, but Hooker had withdrawn into a stronger perimeter that held against their assaults. That morning, though, Hooker suffered a concussion when a cannonball slammed into a post on which he was leaning. He was rendered insensible for a short time and seemed dazed and confused for hours afterward, but he never relinquished command of the army. Whether because of his injury or something else, Hooker not only failed to make the most of his advantage over the divided Army of Northern Virginia, he ordered his men to sit still and wait for Lee to punish them. His only offensive order came later in the day when he called for Sedgwick to cross at Fredericksburg and save him.

Sedgwick moved forward and managed to force Early out of his position at Fredericksburg. He then began to advance toward Lee's rear. Knowing that he could not afford to let this new threat go unchecked, Lee divided his forces yet again. He left a small screening force to watch Hooker, who was still cowering against the river, and turned with the rest of his army to join Early. On May 4, Lee mauled Sedgwick outside Fredericksburg, sending him reeling back over the Rappahannock. On May 5, Lee returned to attack Hooker once more, but by this time Hooker had seen enough and on May 6 he managed to pull his army back over the Rappahannock to safety. With that, perhaps the most amazing of Lee's campaigns ended.

From the perspective of history, Lee had accomplished an incredible feat. Facing an army nearly twice his size, he had divided his forces into mere slivers of what Hooker could bring against him. He then hurled those pieces at just the right times and places to not only survive the battle, but to win a resounding victory that certainly ranks amongst the greatest of this period of world history. People still study Chancellorsville for the sheer power and artistry of Lee's performance there. Lee himself was still not satisfied. When one of his assistants came to give him the news that Hooker had retreated and that the battle had been won, Lee said angrily, "That is the trouble with you young people! You always let those people get away!" (Lee never called the Federals the "enemy." He referred to them simply as "those people.") Lee was not satisfied with simply repulsing Hooker's army; he wanted it destroyed!

After Chancellorsville, Lee never saw Jackson again. For a short time after his operation, Jackson seemed to rally, but pneumonia set in and arrested his improvement. When it became clear that he would not recover, his doctors sent word to Lee to come say good-bye. Lee was already hard at work preparing for the next campaign. He said that he was confident that God would not take Jackson from the Confederacy when it needed him so badly, and that he had prayed for Jackson the previous night as he had never before prayed. He therefore refused to go, apparently taking it as proof of God's provision for his army that Jackson would survive. When Jackson died in spite of Lee's prayers, it shook Lee to his core. Lee believed that the Confederacy could only win independence if God stood with them. The loss of the most Christian general among them, whom Lee needed a great deal, seemed to testify that God had other plans. This realization might have contributed to Lee's almost reckless desire to force a decisive battle in the upcoming months.

After Jackson's death, Lee reorganized his army again, modernizing it this time. It had previously been composed of a number of very large divisions, organized into two wings, one under Jackson and one under Longstreet. This had proved unwieldy and difficult to manage. Now Lee broke the army up into three corps, one under Longstreet, one under A. P. Hill, and one under Richard "Dick" Ewell, an eccentric but heretofore effective division commander who had served Jackson well. The scheme was similar to the one the Federals had used since McClellan, but in the Confederate reckoning, the bodies of men were much larger. For instance, some Confederate divisions were larger than entire Union corps.

As Lee reached the height of his success in Virginia, things were not going so well in the West. Grant was making slow but steady progress in destroying the Confederacy. After his setback at Shiloh, he had driven his opponents into Mississippi. With the fall of New Orleans in 1862, the Confederates controlled only a small section of the Mississippi River that ran from Vicksburg in the north to Port Hudson in the south. Grant set about taking Vicksburg, opposed by John C. Pemberton, who held the city with 30,000 troops, and Johnston, who later arrived with another 25,000. After a number of notable failures, Grant hit upon a plan that worked well. By mid-May he captured Jackson, Mississippi, cutting off Johnston from reinforcing Pemberton. He then turned on Pemberton, beating him in a series of battles that ended with Pemberton bottled up inside of Vicksburg and Johnston hovering nearby, apparently unsure of what to do. It looked like Vicksburg would fall if something decisive were not done quickly.

Davis consulted Lee. Johnston, Longstreet, and Beauregard wanted Lee to assume a defensive position in Virginia while Longstreet's corps and Johnston's forces joined another army under Bragg to defeat

William S. Rosecrans in Tennessee. Once that was accomplished, the combined armies would relieve Vicksburg by attacking Grant. Lee, who disliked the idea of weakening his army and giving up the initiative, argued for another plan. Lee would trust Johnston to concentrate his own forces in the west, while Lee would concentrate in the east. He would then launch a massive invasion of Pennsylvania. The combined pressure of Lee's invasion and the sicknesses of the summer months would be enough to force Grant to leave Vicksburg, and if Lee could win a big enough victory, he could end the war. As usual, Davis was swayed by Lee's logic and ordered him to proceed.

As Lee maneuvered in preparation for the march north, he trusted Stuart to keep his army's movements a secret. On June 9, though, Stuart had been shocked by a sudden onslaught of Federal cavalry at Brandy Station. While earlier in the war the Confederate horsemen had enjoyed such an advantage that they had literally ridden rings around their opponents, as time passed the Federals had steadily improved. They were now nearly equal to Stuart and his men. In a hard fought battle, Stuart managed to hold on, but had to call up Confederate infantry to support him. That alerted Hooker to the fact that Lee was on the move. Worse, the near defeat had stung Stuart's pride. When Lee gave him discretion to choose his route north as long as he protected the army and kept him informed of Hooker's movements, Stuart left only a bare minimum of troopers and embarked with the rest on another attempt to ride around the Union army.

Lee entered the Shenandoah Valley and moved north. He crossed the Potomac River on June 25. Part of his plan was to spread his army out and raid through the northern countryside. He hoped that this would not only allow him to move his army without the need for a supply line, but give him a chance to gather food and forage to be sent south to support the future war effort. Lee was careful to keep up the appearance of perfect gentlemanly behavior. He did punish actual depredations when they occurred; after that, though, the lines got fuzzy. Lee's troops did not "steal" supplies. Instead, they paid for them with paper money, which was by that point as worthless in the Confederacy as it was in the Union, or handed out IOUs to frustrated shopkeepers who saw their entire stock carried off before their eyes. The divisions in front did such a thorough job of cleaning out the countryside that the ones that followed complained there was nothing left to take. All in all, Lee managed to send back enough produce from Pennsylvania that he was able to keep the war in the east going for another year.

The Confederates did another sort of harvesting that they made no pretense of justifying. Whenever they encountered an American of African descent on their march, they treated that person as an escaped slave, regardless of whether they were or not. These men, women, and children were captured and sent back to Virginia as slaves. Whatever Lee, the semi-abolitionist Southerner, thought of this, he did nothing to stop it.

While Lee moved, Hooker maneuvered to keep his army between the Confederates and Washington. He hatched a plan to trap Lee using the troops in the garrison at Harpers Ferry as bait. When Halleck refused to approve the plan, Hooker threatened to resign. Halleck and Lincoln surprised Hooker by accepting his resignation, replacing him with Meade on June 28, only three days before the Battle of Gettysburg. Meade was an experienced army officer who commanded Lee's respect. When Lee heard of the change, he remarked that he must make no mistakes, because Meade would be quick to take advantage of them.

Lee was in a very dangerous position, even though he did not know it. At one point, the vanguard of his army was well into Pennsylvania while the rear guard was still in Virginia. This left him very thin at many points, and if Hooker could strike him before Lee could concentrate his army, the Army of Northern Virginia might well be destroyed. Lee trusted the normally reliable Stuart to keep him notified of the position of the Union army. This time, his trust was misplaced. When Stuart embarked on his latest attempt to ride around the Union army, he discovered that the new and improved Union cavalry were up to the task of hunting him. They cut him off from Lee and kept him on the run. Stuart was unable to join Lee again until July 2, and then was not able to contribute much to the battle. Fortunately, a scout brought Lee the shocking news that the Union army was closer to parts of Lee's force than those parts were to each other. Lee ordered an immediate concentration at Cashtown, Pennsylvania, just west of a road hub named Gettysburg.

Lee issued orders for his troops to avoid conflict with the enemy until his forces had fully assembled. He did not want to risk losing a part of his army before the rest of it could get there. Meade, who was still trying to gain control of his own army, had issued similar orders on June 30, but those orders did not reached cavalry commander John Buford or corps commander John Reynolds. They made the decision to hold Gettysburg, and when a Confederate division led by Henry Heth marched down the Chambersburg Pike toward town, Buford put up stiff resistance and called on Reynolds for reinforcements. Heth, thinking that his division could easily defeat a cavalry detachment, escalated the fight and had nearly won when Reynolds's First Corps arrived and the fight turned into a full-fledged battle.

Lee was furious when he heard firing in the distance; significant portions of his army were still en route. He was initially inclined to pull his men back until he learned that Ewell, coming back from Carlisle in the north, would be arriving directly on the Federal flank. Lee could hardly have asked for a better situation had he planned it, and he ordered everyone forward. The Union lines held for most of the day but collapsed almost simultaneously at all points late that afternoon. The victorious Confederates chased the Army of the Potomac through town and onto a series of ridges to the south.

Meade's line that was then forming quickly took on the appearance of what many historians have since described as a giant fish hook, with the curved end pointing north. An alternative description might be a cane or shepherd's crook. The "barb" of the fishhook started at Culp's Hill, moved north and west onto Cemetery Hill, and then turned sharply south following Cemetery Ridge until it culminated on two prominent hills called the Round Tops. Lee's army took up positions opposite them, in town and along Seminary Ridge, approximately one mile away. Meade had about 95,000 men, while Lee commanded approximately 75,000.

As evening fell, Lee noted that Cemetery Hill and Culp's Hill were key to the Union position. He also saw that they seemed to be lightly defended. Lee sent word to Ewell, asking him to press forward and take the heights "if possible." Ewell, who was more used to the clear, direct orders given by Jackson as opposed to Lee's suggestions, did nothing. Overnight, the Federals reinforced the hills, ending any hope of an easy victory, if there had really ever been one at all.

That night, Longstreet approached Lee with a suggestion of his own, one that he had made before. Longstreet argued that they should disengage and move around Meade to the south. If they could get between Meade and Washington, they could wait for Meade to attack them on ground of their own choosing. In effect, Longstreet wanted to try to recreate Fredericksburg. Lee listened to him, but decided against it. Lee seemed more interested in recreating Chancellorsville. They had already won the first day's fighting, and he worried if he marched away that it would result in a serious morale problem for his army. Also, Lee was dedicated to maintaining the initiative. The Army of the Potomac was on the field at Gettysburg, and so at Gettysburg he would attack them. He ordered Longstreet to prepare an attack on the Federal left flank to go in the next day. He did not order Longstreet to attack at dawn, as some postwar accounts have alleged. He sent word for Ewell to attack Culp's Hill and Cemetery Hill to distract Meade and prevent him from sending reinforcements to his left. Longstreet left, but apparently did not accept Lee's orders as serious.

The next morning, Lee checked on Ewell, but awaited news of Longstreet's advance. When nothing happened, he sought out Longstreet and found that his "Old War Horse" had done nothing to prepare for the assault. It was then 11:00 A.M. Lee positively ordered Longstreet to attack. After five more hours of feet dragging, Longstreet finally got into position and launched his assault. When an opportunity presented itself to flank the Union army, Longstreet refused, claiming that he would follow Lee's orders to the letter, even though Lee would surely have blessed the movement as an example of good generalship.

In effect, Longstreet was implementing what amounted to a self-fulfilling prophecy. He had told Lee that fighting at Gettysburg would lead to failure, Lee had refused to listen, and now Longstreet proceeded to fight as if defeat were a foregone conclusion. Along the way, Longstreet himself contributed quite a bit to the cause of Confederate defeat by delaying the action, arguing with his commander, and "saving lives" by not committing all the troops he could have, when those troops could have made the difference between victory and defeat. Lee contributed to the problem by refusing to confront Longstreet. Indeed, his fear of confrontation had created the problem by encouraging Longstreet to believe that he, and not Lee, was the stronger personality and therefore in de facto command of the army.

Longstreet's men fought viciously across Devil's Den, the Peach Orchard, the Wheat Field, and Little Round Top. Though they experienced temporary success later in the afternoon, Meade transferred troops from his right and repulsed the attack. Darkness ended the fighting on Lee's right, but not his left. Ewell's attack finally went in about nightfall and, thanks to a mistake on Meade's part, he managed to wrest control of much of Culp's Hill away from the Union. An indecisive night battle followed, but by midnight Meade had reinforced his position, limiting the usefulness of Lee's gains there.

That night, Lee decided to make another daring gamble. He thought that since he had struck both ends of the Union army, Meade must have moved troops out to reinforce them. If he attacked Meade's center with a powerful stroke, he might be able to break it. The division of George E. Pickett had just arrived on the battlefield and was fresh. Lee ordered Longstreet to use Pickett for the attack, with a few additions and substitutions from A. P. Hill's corps, giving him a force of approximately 15,000 men. Ewell would attack Culp's Hill again as a distraction and Stuart would try to cause trouble in the rear of the army. Longstreet once again resisted. He told Lee that he had been in the army a long time and that "I think I can safely say there never was a body of fifteen thousand men who could make that attack successfully." Lee dismissed Longstreet impatiently, insisting that he follow orders and attack in the morning.

The attack would be difficult, but was not as hopeless as Longstreet seemed to think. The biggest problem was the lay of the land. Longstreet's men would have to cross a mile of rolling terrain in full view of the Federal line, particularly the Round Tops, with virtually no cover. Lee planned to soften the Union line with a massive artillery bombardment first, one that would prove to be the largest yet seen on the North American continent. If the guns were successful, 15,000 men should be enough to rush across the ground and win the decisive victory Lee wanted. It certainly was no more ridiculous to believe such a thing was possible than it was to suggest that what Lee had previously done to Pope, Burnside, or Hooker would work. If Pickett could pierce the line and hold his position, Meade's army would disintegrate in confusion and could perhaps be destroyed.

As the sun rose on July 3, 1863, Lee rode with Longstreet and Pickett to oversee the final details of the assault. Unfortunately, Ewell attacked at daylight and his men fought themselves out long before Longstreet was ready. At 1:00 P.M., Lee ordered the bombardment to begin, focusing on a small copse of trees just behind the line where Pickett's troops were to attack. Alexander, now Longstreet's chief of artillery, opened fire with 159 guns, and an equally large number of Union guns responded. The bombardment had continued for almost an hour when Alexander thought he saw a slackening in the Union return fire. The Union gun crews seemed to be pulling their guns out of line. If Pickett attacked quickly, he might make it across the field before they came back. Alexander began to run low on ammunition. He notified Longstreet, but Longstreet did not want to take responsibility for what was happening and refused to give the order to advance. A few minutes later Alexander sent word to Pickett, "For God's sake come quick. . . . Come quick or my ammunition will not let me support you properly."

Pickett gave the note to Longstreet, who still did nothing. Finally, Pickett asked, "General, shall I advance?" Longstreet nodded and Pickett saluted, replying that he was moving forward before galloping off.

Chapter 6

THE TIDE RECEDES

When Longstreet gave his final agreement for Lee's last attack at Gettysburg, George Pickett turned to his soldiers, shouting, "Up, men, and to your posts! Don't forget today that you are from old Virginia!" Porter Alexander's guns fell silent as Pickett's troops passed through them to charge across the mile of open ground separating the Union and Confederate lines. The men formed up into beautiful ranks, out in the open in front of both armies. When the advance began, both sides thought it looked more like a dress parade than an attack. The Federal soldiers awaiting them were in awe of the spectacle. For many, that moment seemed frozen in time.

The magic was shattered by the crash and thunder of dozens of Federal cannon coming back into the fray. While Alexander had believed that his bombardment had succeeded in silencing Meade's artillery, most of his shots had flown too high. They had pummeled the rear of the army (including Meade's headquarters) but had done little damage to the line itself. Union artillery commander Henry Hunt had instead ordered his guns to fall silent at intervals and to refresh their supplies, giving the false impression that the Confederates were winning. His renewed guns opened with a roar from all over the Union line, throwing up dirt and body parts wherever they struck the advancing Confederates. When Pickett's troops got close enough, Hunt's men switched to firing canister, ammunition that essentially turned their cannons into giant shotguns capable of mowing down dozens in a single shot. Still, the Confederates came on. When they advanced into range of the Union infantry, the entire Federal line erupted in a sheet of flame. Rows of men fell in line, knocked over like bowling pins. The Confederates fired back and kept moving forward.

Convinced the attack was doomed from the beginning, Longstreet had kept some supporting troops back that he should have included, and this made it possible for Union regiments on both sides of Pickett's attack to wheel out of line and fire into his flanks, punishing him on three sides. Still, the Confederates advanced. They actually pierced the Army of the Potomac's center and for a short time there was hand-to-hand fighting. It would not last. Fresh Union reinforcements arrived and charged into the battle, pushing the Confederate survivors back out. The few who remained tried to retreat back across the mile of ground, with Federals shooting at them and shouting "Fredericksburg! Fredericksburg!" Lee's biggest gambled had failed, and Longstreet had his defeat.

Lee had watched the charge develop from Seminary Ridge, later joining Alexander in his advanced position. Through the smoke he was able to follow the course of the action, and knew what had happened. As the wounded streamed back from the desolation, Lee tried to comfort them and get them ready to repel the counterattack he expected from Meade. "All this will come right in the end," he said. "We'll talk it over afterwards; but, in the meantime, all good men must rally." He took full responsibility for the failure on himself: "[A]ll this has been my fault—it is I that have lost this fight and you must help me out of it the best way you can."

Meade's counterattack never materialized. His army had been so mauled by victory that he was as badly in need of rest as were Lee and his men. Unfortunately for Lee, rest was not an option. He had to organize a retreat back to Virginia and safety immediately. That night, Lee was so exhausted that he was almost unable to dismount Traveller. John Imboden, one of Lee's cavalry commanders, tried to help him, but Lee managed to get down on his own, and for some time simply leaned against his horse, a grieved expression on his face. Lee told Imboden that he "never saw troops behave more magnificently than Pickett's division of Virginians did to-day. . . . And if they had been supported as they were to have been . . . we would have held the position and the day would have been ours." Lee then said in a loud voice, "Too bad! *Too bad! OH TOO BAD!*"

It was indeed Lee's fault. Whatever the flaws of Longstreet, Stuart, and Ewell, Lee placed them in their positions; he tolerated their behavior and was ultimately responsible for making sure that they did not negatively affect the operations of the army. In part, his own failure came from his persona and the command style that had developed from it. He did not take a strong hand with his men or bring their personalities under control. He preferred to suggest and deflect rather than order and confront. In the end, Lee was simply human; he made mistakes, and at Gettysburg he paid for them. His army suffered somewhere between 20,000 and 28,000 casualties. Lee had lost one-third of his entire force.

Of course it is important not to forget that there were two armies on the field that day. Historians have so focused on the Confederates and what they did and did not do at Gettysburg that they often overlook the fact that for all that Lee and his generals did wrong, there was quite

The dead after the Battle of Gettysburg. (National Archives.)

a bit that Meade did right. It is not enough to ask, "How did Lee lose Gettysburg?" without asking "How did Meade win it?" When Pickett himself was asked after the war who was to blame for Lee's failure that day he simply and accurately replied that he thought the Yankees had something to do with it.

Both of the major eastern armies sat still on July 4, tending to their wounded and preparing for the next moves, but to the west important events were afoot. On that day, Vicksburg surrendered to Grant. With the fall of Port Hudson not long after, the entire Mississippi River was back under Federal control. As the news made its way east in the wake of Meade's victory at Gettysburg, Northern morale rose significantly. While generations of historians looked at Gettysburg as the "high tide of the Confederacy," it was in reality simply one more receding wave on the beach. Lee had surged forward and was now retreating. In the meantime, Grant was systematically disassembling the Confederacy and gradually progressing farther and farther east. Lee's victories were not winning the war, but they were prolonging it. In hindsight, Gettysburg was not the Confederacy's high tide, but it was Lee's.

Lee's retreat began in earnest on July 4, and it was a horrible affair. The army had taken as many wounded as it could pile on the wagons, and those men suffered terribly. Their screams echoed along the road, many of them begging to die or calling for loved ones they would never see again. The trains were deluged by pounding rains that bogged wagons down and slowed the retreat to a crawl. The only blessing was that Meade did not seem to be fully over the terror of Lee that had plagued Federal commanders. His pursuit was so tentative that one Confederate officer described it as "a mule goes chasing a grizzly bear—as if catching up with us was the last thing he wanted to do." Apart from being harassed by Judson Kilpatrick's cavalry, Lee's army managed to make it across the Potomac on July 14. The Army of Northern Virginia had lived to fight another day.

In the wake of Gettysburg, Lee took a hard look at himself and his prospects for winning the war. Any chance that Lee seemed to think he had of winning the war by a bold, powerful stroke he believed lost at Gettysburg. His army was recovering very slowly, and Lee had to resort to firing squads to curtail desertion. Many in the Confederate press seemed to agree and turned on Lee, printing critical articles that often involved far more reporting than investigation, given how few facts the journalists apparently had available to them. Lee's own health was worsening, and he found himself "more and more incapable of exertion." He therefore offered to resign in light of his recent failure. Davis responded, "To ask me to substitute you by some one in my judgment more fit to command . . . is to demand an impossibility." He implored Lee to "take all possible care of yourself." Davis, and the Confederacy, was dedicated to Lee.

The fall of 1863 saw both eastern armies weakened in order to strengthen those in the west. First, Davis faced a crisis. He had already lost Vicksburg, and Rosecrans's army in Tennessee significantly outnumbered Bragg's men. Rosecrans, a careful commander, was steadily maneuvering Bragg out of the state. Bragg tried on several occasions to mount attacks, but the high command of his army had become a viper pit of insubordination where his chief officers actually taught weekly courses on military policy to their men chiefly to explain why Bragg, their commander, was an idiot. They routinely refused to obey Bragg's orders, and Bragg, who was perhaps one of the worst leaders in the Confederacy, could not handle them. Though Davis inexplicably chose to retain both Bragg and his antagonists, he did send reinforcements from Lee's army to try to tip the scales in Bragg's favor. Davis detached Longstreet's corps and sent him to Bragg. In his absence, Lee would face Meade with only about 47,000 men.

Bragg was able to successfully resume the offensive and he attacked Rosecrans at Chickamauga, on the northern border of Georgia near Chattanooga, Tennessee, on September 19 and 20. Longstreet's men were the ones who actually pierced the Federal line, and one-half of Rosecrans's army disintegrated. The other half remained intact and covered the retreat back to Chattanooga. Bragg caught up and laid siege to Rosecrans, while Longstreet embarked on a pointless campaign to Knoxville, Tennessee. Lee would have to operate without his "Old War Horse" until he finally wandered back into his stall in April 1864.

In the meantime, Lincoln relieved Meade of some of his own force. In response to Rosecrans's investment in Chattanooga, Lincoln took two small corps from the Army of the Potomac and sent them west under Joe Hooker. He placed Grant in command of the entire effort, and charged him with saving Rosecrans's army. Over the next few months,

Grant did exactly that, breaking Bragg's hold over the city and pushing him back into Georgia to wait for the opening of the spring campaigns.

Meade came out against Lee with about 77,000 men while the battles and maneuvering for Chattanooga took place. Lee responded by trying to slip his army around Meade's flank to get between him and Washington. Lee was again sick with a "heavy cold" and suffered from considerable chest pain. He felt too ill to ride for part of the campaign. Meade responded by pulling his army back quickly, and Lee tried to strike before he could get away. A. P. Hill thought he had caught a portion of the Third Corps at Bristoe Station and pushed ahead with the reckless abandon that had served Lee and Jackson so well, only to be ambushed by an entire Federal corps waiting in a railroad cut. Hill's men were thrashed, and by the time Lee arrived, the fight was over. He lost 1,300 men and had gained nothing. Rather than continue the fight, Meade withdrew the rest of the way, ending the campaign.

Meade tried again in late November. He ordered an advance across the Rapidan River, hoping to divide Lee's army and destroy each part separately. Lee was ready, though, and prepared a fortified line along Mine Run Creek. Meade discovered Lee on November 28, and began preparations to attack. Then, without warning, Meade called off the assault on December 1, afraid that Lee's lines were too strong. Lee tried to take the initiative himself on December 2, but when his men charged forward, they found Meade's position empty—he had retreated the day before.

Lee's strategy in the Mine Run campaign would essentially remain the same for the rest of the war. His army was small and he knew it would get no bigger. He therefore turned to the tactical use of fortifications to even the odds. Rather than simply look at entrenchments as long-term endeavors used to defend static positions, like Richmond, Lee began to throw them up almost every time he stopped. Mine Run also probably reminded Lee of a conclusion he had already drawn: His last real chance to win the war in Virginia had slipped away. Meade would not make the mistakes of his predecessors.

After the end of the Mine Run campaign, Lee was summoned to Richmond. It appeared that he would be leaving Virginia altogether. He confided to Stuart that he expected to be transferred to Georgia to take command of the army then licking its wounds at Dalton. Lee would obey orders, but he emphatically did not want to be transferred, and approached Richmond as if headed to an execution. Once there, Lee was again able to prevail upon Davis to change his mind. Davis appointed Johnston instead and sent Lee back to the Army of Northern Virginia.

While in Richmond, Lee was finally able to visit his family at their latest home, a small house on Leigh Street. He had not seen Mary for seven months, but the reunion was bittersweet. Mary's condition had worsened significantly and her frustration and pain had begun to affect her judgment. Lee began to treat her more like a child than a wife at times. Rooney Lee was absent. He had been captured while recovering from a wound he had suffered at Brandy Station and was languishing in prison at Ft. Monroe. Rooney's wife, Charlotte, whom Lee adored and called "Chass," was ill, and by that time it was clear she would not recover. When Lee left, he knew it would most likely be the last time he saw her. The Federals had finally formalized the seizure of Arlington, leaving the Lees nothing but thousands of worthless Confederate bonds to call their own. He was able to visit with the rest of his family, and though the war's costs were evident everywhere, so was the good will of those who remained.

Lee was not the only commander who faced a change in position that winter. After Grant's success in Chattanooga, Lincoln decided that he had indeed found his general. Congress resurrected the long-neglected rank of lieutenant general, last held by George Washington, and bestowed it upon Grant. Lincoln placed him in command of all Union armies and tasked him with coordinating the upcoming campaign of 1864.

Both Grant and Lincoln saw and understood what had enabled the Confederacy to survive as long as it had in the face of what should have been overwhelming opposition: poor coordination among the various Union efforts. Each army and each theater had essentially been left to run itself and none ever took the others into account. The Federal armies were, as Grant put it, "like a balky team [of oxen], no two ever pulling together." This had allowed the Confederates to shift their forces from one place to another, always just in time to meet the newest crises. Grant proposed launching a massive offensive of all armies together. If done properly, the offensive would leave the Confederates overwhelmed and unable to react. According to Lincoln's frontier analogy, "those not skinning can hold a leg."

Grant appointed William T. Sherman to command Rosecrans's former army in Tennessee facing Johnston in Georgia. Sherman, a high-strung, intelligent man, had been working with Grant since early in the war, and had provided him with an ideal military partner. In Virginia, Grant constructed three armies for simultaneous operation against Lee. Franz Sigel (later, David Hunter) would advance down the Shenandoah Valley, denying it to the Confederates. Benjamin Butler would lead an army inland from the coast to attack Richmond from the east and south. Grant himself would oversee Meade and the Army of the Potomac in an advance against Lee from the north. This created an awkward situation in which Meade was still technically in command of his own army, but had no ultimate tactical or strategic control over it with Grant there. Both in Georgia and Virginia, the goal of the main army would be to destroy its Confederate counterparts by pinning them against cities they would not abandon—Atlanta and Richmond—and then pounding them into oblivion. The smaller, supporting forces would prevent Davis from sending reinforcements.

The army that Lee had used to defend the Old Dominion against Grant hardly resembled the one he had commanded the year before, and he was not sure of the quality of his commanders. Of the brigade and division commanders Lee had led in 1863, roughly half had been killed, transferred, or promoted into new positions where they remained unproven. Of his corps commanders, only Longstreet seemed capable, and he of course had his own issues. Both Ewell, whose performance had fallen off dramatically since losing a leg and marrying a childhood sweetheart, and Hill, who had suffered from gonorrhea or yellow fever for years and was in precarious health, could be very questionable. Lee was also outnumbered, as usual. In mid-April, he estimated his army to be about 64,000 strong, while Meade still commanded over 75,000 troops. Lee would increase his force to about 70,000, but he had no hope of matching Grant, who eventually moved with 120,000 men, plus cavalry and artillery.

On May 4, Lee reported to Davis that the Army of the Potomac was on the move and had crossed the Rapidan River into the Wilderness once again. Grant and Meade intended to push rapidly through and force Lee to fight in the open somewhere farther south. Lee wanted to hit Grant before he could get clear, once again using the Wilderness as an equalizing factor. He ordered Ewell to make a probing attack on May 5, though he did not want to bring on a full-scale battle until his entire army had reached the field. When Ewell's men collided with the Army of the Potomac, Grant and Meade decided to attack immediately, hoping to destroy Lee in spite of their disadvantages. After several failed attempts, both sides started entrenching. To the south, Hill's men almost succeeded in seizing a key road intersection, but the Federals held on, setting the stage for the next day's fighting.

On the morning of May 6, Major General Winfield Scott Hancock launched a massive assault against the center of Lee's line. It stretched and then broke. In desperation, Lee rushed to the front on Traveller to rally his men. Just then, the first of Longstreet's troops arrived, and Lee turned to them to seal the breach. When it became apparent that he intended to lead them himself, Lee's men refused to go forward unless he went back behind them to safety. "Go back!" they shouted, "Lee to the rear!" For a while, Lee did not seem to hear them. He looked set on charging, perhaps to his death. Finally, a member of his staff caught hold of Traveller's reins and forcibly led Lee away. Longstreet took over and stabilized the front.

Later in the day, Longstreet found a route into the southern flank of Hancock's forces, and personally led an assault that crushed it. Longstreet himself was wounded badly and the attack stalled. Almost one year after Lee had lost his "right arm" in the Wilderness, his "Old War Horse" fell there too. Though Longstreet would survive, his recovery was a long, slow process and it deprived Lee of his most trusted commander when he needed him desperately. When Lee later renewed the attack, Hancock's men had constructed breastworks and repulsed Lee's men easily. Meanwhile, the Confederates had found a way to strike the exposed northern flank of Grant's army. Late in the afternoon, Lee sent John B. Gordon's division forward. Gordon crashed into the line and routed part of it, but darkness fell, ending the fighting and allowing the Federals the chance to reinforce.

Even though the fighting ended in a tactical draw, it was another excellent performance for Lee. Over the course of two days, he had stopped a much superior army by attacking it at a place that gave him far more advantages than it did his enemies. The next day, he had managed to survive a powerful stroke and then hit back and partially rout both flanks of the Army of the Potomac. Unfortunately, he paid for it. Longstreet was gone for the foreseeable future and Lee had lost 11,000 men. True, he had caused the Federals 17,000 casualties, but Grant could replace his losses while Lee could not.

All of the previous commanders Lee had faced would most likely have retreated after facing such punishment, and Lee would have been given some time to at least rest his army. Grant was a very different man. He preferred to win by strategy and movement, and therefore with a minimal loss of life, but if that did not work, Grant was determined enough to use all of his resources to keep fighting. For his part, Lee understood Grant and what he could do. Lee respected Grant's abilities and did not take the grandiose risks he had against men like McClellan, Pope, and Hooker. He played his hand conservatively and matched Grant move for move.

Grant believed that Lee's lines were too strong to assault, but instead of retreating, he advanced. He moved his army to the southeast, attempting to get between Lee and Richmond. Lee had ridden the length of his lines several times after the end of the battle and had deduced Grant's next move. When he heard that the Union army was in motion, he placed his own on the road to Spotsylvania Courthouse. It quickly became a race to see who could get there first.

Along the way, Lee lost another commander, at least temporarily. Hill's continuing illness had taken a turn for the worse and he had been forced to give up his corps command. He could not ride a horse and in fact could hardly walk. He was following his troops in an ambulance. Lee appointed Jubal Early in his stead, but he had now lost two of his three corps commanders and had little confidence in the ability of Ewell, the last one remaining.

Grant almost won the race, but Lee's cavalry fought an important delaying action at Todd's Tavern during the night of May 7–8. That bought just enough time for Longstreet's replacement, Richard Anderson, to get to the crossroads. Uncoordinated attacks by Grant's First and Sixth Corps were not enough to dislodge Anderson, and the rest of both armies arrived for the next stage of the campaign.

On May 9, Lee laid out his line and started his men digging in with a vengeance. His position would eventually stretch for over seven miles. Due to the shape of the terrain, it featured a huge protrusion toward the Federal army at one point, called a "salient." The Confederates jokingly referred to the area as the "Mule Shoe" because that was what it somewhat resembled. Lee planned to straighten his lines and get rid of it, but in the meantime he posted Ewell's entire corps there and supported him with a large amount of artillery. Also on that day, Grant's cavalry commander, Phillip Sheridan, embarked on a raid toward Richmond with 10,000 cavalry. Stuart left to chase him the next morning.

On May 10, Grant attacked Lee's line in force, but was bloodily repulsed. A smaller attack on the "Mule Shoe" saw some limited success. It pierced Ewell's lines, but did not have enough force to exploit the break, and the Federals had to retreat. Grant took note of it though, and used that information to plan his next move.

Grant shuffled his troops around on May 11 in preparation for his coming assault. This led Lee to believe that the Army of the Potomac was about to move again. Lee ordered much of his artillery limbered up and taken out of line, particularly around the Mule Shoe. When Grant's massive attack hit the salient on May 12, Ewell was much weaker than he had been before. By the time Lee heard what was going on, Federal forces had penetrated deeply into the Mule Shoe and were close to achieving a decisive victory. Once again, Lee personally led troops toward the crisis and was ready to take them into the fight himself. Once again, the troops shouted "Lee to the rear! For God's sake, go back!" and refused to charge until Lee had agreed to return to safety. They then countercharged the Federals and pushed them back enough to rob them of total victory.

The fighting in the Mule Shoe—by now also called the "Bloody Angle"—was some of war's most intense. Thousands of men spent hours grappling with each other, separated by only a few feet of earth. A man would jump up on the parapet, shoot his rifle into the enemy below, and then throw it like spear, only to be handed another gun to repeat the process until he had been shot down and someone else had taken his place. Meanwhile, Lee hastily constructed a new, contracted line behind the Bloody Angle. His men held on until nightfall, when they were able to fall back onto the new position and abandon the deadly ground they had fought over all day. Lee's faithful adjutant, Taylor, called it "the most remarkable musketry-fire of the war: from the sides of the salient in possession of the Federals, and the new line . . . occupied by the Confederates, poured forth hissing fire, an incessant, terrific hail. No living man nor thing could stand in the doomed space . . . even large trees were felled—their trunks cut in twain by the bullets of small arms."

Lee himself nearly became one of the casualties. While Lee was ordering his troops forward and they were again ordering him to the rear, Traveller reared for some reason. Lee kept his saddle, but at that precise moment, a cannonball passed underneath his prized horse's stomach, missing it by only inches. Had Traveller not chosen that instant to rear, both he and his proud rider would likely have died.

May 12 brought even more bad news for Lee. J.E.B. Stuart had won his race against Sheridan and waited for him at Yellow Tavern. Sheridan attacked on May 11, and during the afternoon's fighting, Stuart had been shot in the stomach and carried to Richmond. Stuart died the next day, after stating simply that he wished God's will to be done and joining in singing the old hymn, "Rock of Ages." Grieving for Stuart, Lee called him, "an ardent, brave, & devoted soldier" that "never brought me a false piece of information." Lee was watching his military family die one after the other, and he knew that he could never replace Stuart any more than he could Jackson. He increasingly relied on a younger group of commanders, Gordon foremost among them.

These losses perhaps caused Lee to take the chances with his life that he now did. Lee had never been frightened away from the front lines by the threat of death, but he also knew that his duty called him to coordinate the army and that was most effectively handled from the rear. Since the Wilderness, though, Lee seemed intent on not only going to the front, but personally leading deadly charges into the teeth of the enemy. Why he did so is still debated, but it was probably a combination of influences. Lee knew how desperate these situations were. If each crisis were not contained, then Lee would have no army left to command. With so many of his commanders falling, Lee had no one else to trust at moments like that, and felt he must see to them personally. Finally, Lee saw the approaching end of the war and he saw his own health and that of his family failing. It may be that he wanted, in some way, to die a glorious death in battle rather than wait for a Federal hangman or old age to catch him.

Grant soon tried to renew the offensive. He attempted to slip a large force around to attack Lee's right flank on May 13 and do to him what Lee had done to others so often before. The steady, heavy rain that started the day before continued for four days, slowed Grant down, and gave Lee ample opportunity to counter him. When the attack went in on May 14, Lee's troops repulsed the Army of the Potomac handily. Grant's next attempt came on May 18 when he renewed the battle in the Bloody Angle sector, but this time Ewell easily beat back his attacks. On May 19, Lee made a foray of his own. He ordered Ewell to move forward to make sure Grant was not trying to slip around them again and to feel out the Union right flank. Ewell was repulsed after a fight, but he did find Grant still in place.

On May 20, Grant was on the move again, to the south and east, once more trying to put his army between Lee and Richmond. Lee managed to outrace Grant again, this time to the North Anna River which he reached on May 22. There, Lee set up an ingenious defensive position that forced Grant to split his army into three separate parts, each one separated from the other by the river. Lee was desperate to regain the initiative, and when Grant advanced into his trap, it seemed his chance had come.

Unfortunately, on May 24, Lee himself fell seriously ill with a sickness that affected his bowels. He could not leave camp and spent most of his time on his cot venting his anger at his inability to act. He could not himself lead the attack and he had no one he could trust to do it for him. Hill had reported back for duty on May 21, but was obviously still sick. Ewell, too, was having trouble and could not be counted on. Grant soon realized the danger and pulled back, robbing Lee of possibly his last chance to strike a serious blow. The Army of the Potomac took the roads toward Richmond, and Lee, still feeling ill, raced his men ahead of it. He set up new lines along Totopotomoy Creek, only nine miles from Richmond. For the first time in the campaign, he also made his headquarters in a house, where he could rest more comfortably.

While here, Lee pressed Davis for any troops he could spare. Davis sent him Pickett's division, which had been detached on service to the James River, and troops from the valley. Lee also asked that he be sent men from P.G.T. Beauregard's army south of Richmond. Beauregard had fought a tight campaign against the army under Butler attacking Richmond from the southeast, and by this time had bottled them up neatly. Beauregard did not take kindly to Lee's request and initially tried to argue with him, but Lee wrote to Davis warning that there would be a "disaster" if his orders were not heeded. Davis immediately backed Lee and ordered the transfer of part of Beauregard's army. He left the rest intact, watching the Federals near Petersburg. Lee extended his lines and looked for any chance to strike at Grant and push him away from Richmond. If something were not done, he expected Grant to force a siege of Richmond. If that happened, Lee knew that it would be only a matter of time.

On May 30, Lee tried another attack using Jubal Early, now in command of a corps. He assaulted the Union Fifth Corps in the vicinity of Bethesda Church on the far left of the Union army. Anderson, who was supposed to coordinate with Early, failed to attack and the battle ended inconclusively after hard fighting on both sides.

Grant decided to switch tactics. He had been moving around Lee's flank for a month, but had made no clear progress toward his goal of destroying him. Lee's lines were once again strung out along a seven-mile front and, given the casualties of the past few weeks, Grant theorized that Lee might be weak in the middle. He massed his forces for a huge attack aimed at Cold Harbor. At this point in time, Cold Harbor was neither "cold" nor was it anywhere near a "harbor." It drew its name from a local tavern where travelers could purchase a room for the night but not food. The armies had actually fought over that ground before; Cold Harbor was in the same vicinity as Gaines's Mill, where Lee had won his single victory of the Seven Days' Battles in 1862. A little known alternative name for the fight at Gaines's Mill was First Cold Harbor. Grant now looked to launch a battle there that would dwarf anything 1862 had seen.

In the meantime, Lee was examining all of his lines and personally directing their fortification. With his reinforcements from Richmond, Lee was able to fully man his position, though he was still offensive minded enough to be ever on the lookout for another chance to attack. By the time Grant was ready to launch, Lee's line was one of the strongest he had yet produced. Grant would be sending his men into the very worst of it.

On the morning of June 2, Grant's men prepared to die. By this point in the campaign they had come to expect slaughter, and none of them thought they would survive the day. Many of them scribbled their names and addresses onto scraps of paper and pinned them to their coats so their bodies could be identified after the battle and their families could know what had become of them. It was certainly a far cry from the atmosphere of jubilation with which some of them had marched off to join the "short" and "glorious" war four years before.

The storm of war broke at 4:30 A.M. Three large columns of attackers poured over the ground between the two armies. Lee's men simply mowed them down by the thousands. At points, the Federals were 28 men deep and all pressed constantly forward. The Confederates hunkered down behind their entrenchments and poured fire directly into the Federals' faces, while the artillery fired loads of double canister, wiping out dozens at a time. Men were being struck by two and three balls at once and the survivors fell down where they stood, trying to lay as low as they could among the dead and dying. Grant lost 7,000 men in the first hour of the fighting alone. By midday, the attack orders were still coming from headquarters, but by that point the men in the ranks simply refused to obey them. Finally, Grant ordered the attacks suspended. The men who survived had to dig in where they were and they began the same trench-to-trench fighting they had begun at Spotsylvania.

Generals are in the business of sending men to their deaths. They may not desire it, but in fact they must be willing to give such orders if they are to succeed and defeat their enemies. There is, therefore, a certain amount of guilt that must be accepted as part of part of the job. Cold Harbor was something new to Grant, however. That evening, Grant wrote that, "I regret this assault more than any one I have ever ordered. I regarded it as a stern necessity; but, as it has proved, no advantages have been gained sufficient to justify the losses suffered." His losses would have been hard to justify in the best of circumstances. Of the 15,500 total casualties for the battle, only 2,500 came from Lee's army. An incredible 13,000 Federal troops fell in about six hours of fighting. Cold Harbor so wrecked the morale of Grant's army that historians have since referred to something called "Cold Harbor Syndrome," a pathological fear among troops of attacking prepared positions. After Cold Harbor, they simply would not do it and Grant had to change his strategy and tactics to compensate.

While historians talk about this or that battle of what has come to be called the "Overland Campaign" of 1864, in a very real sense the action of the previous month was simply one long battle drawn out across a space of time that would have been thought absurd only a few years before. The two armies came into contact with each other and stayed in contact almost constantly from the Wilderness through Cold Harbor. When not actively engaging in serious hostilities, they fought what amounted to a continual skirmish from point to point.

The results had been devastating to both armies. Grant had lost upwards of 50,000 men since the campaign began or roughly 1,700 men per day on average. Lee had lost fewer men—around 32,000—but that had to be deducted from a much smaller army and translated into about half the force he started with in on May 4. On June 4, two very different armies faced each other, in a quite literal sense. Almost half of each had been killed or wounded. Grant was able to replace his losses with new regiments, but Lee could not come close to recouping his. Even with the troops Davis had sent, Lee's army shrank by the day, forcing him to rely more and more on entrenchments.

Another effect of the armies no longer maneuvering as before was that the dead and wounded remained in the no man's land between the two forces. Whereas before the armies would move on and people—often locals—would come out to help the injured and bury the dead, at Cold Harbor the wounded and dying simply rotted where they lay. Two days passed before Grant and Lee worked out a truce to allow for unarmed burial teams to start to work. By that time, many more had died and the stench had become overpowering. When they began searching on June 7, they found only four men still alive on that vast field of death.

Lee next expected Grant to begin his long awaited, longer feared movement south of the James River to attack Petersburg. He kept a sharp watch for Grant's movements, but did not see any evidence demonstrating that Grant had actually started. Down in Petersburg, Beauregard still had command of the forces watching the Federals he had bottled up earlier in Bermuda Neck. By this point in the war, Beauregard had disgusted both Davis and Lee, and neither seemed willing to trust his judgment. He had lost Davis's confidence by taking a long sick leave to recover from an illness, something that the hard driving Davis thought unconscionable in time of war. He had lost Lee's by his consistent refusal to cooperate, especially as the armies had neared Richmond.

So when Beauregard began reporting increased Federal activity in his sector, Davis and Lee dismissed his reports as simple overreaction. When he said that more transports had been sighted in the river, no one really believed he was seeing what he thought he was seeing. By June 15, Beauregard had come under attack, though he was able to hold his position. Over the course of the next three days, the attacks intensified, and Beauregard grew more insistent that something was wrong. By June 18, Lee had finally accepted that Grant had shifted his troops to the south side of the James, and he rushed to get to Beauregard in time. Though it was another close race, Beauregard managed to hold on until Lee reached him.

The siege of Petersburg had begun.

Chapter 7

"A STILLNESS AT APPOMATTOX"

Petersburg, Virginia, is located about 25 miles south of Richmond on the Appomattox River. It lies roughly 10 miles upriver from where the Appomattox meets the James east of Richmond. According to the 1860 census, about 18,000 people lived in Petersburg, and half of them were black. Petersburg might have been somewhat unremarkable in most other circumstances, but since Richmond had become the wartime capital of the Confederacy, it had become a place people were willing to die to keep or obtain. In a very real and strategic sense, Petersburg was the gateway to Richmond. Two railroads key to keeping the capital supplied and connected to the rest of the country, the Weldon and the Southside, converged at Petersburg before proceeding into Richmond. If Grant could take Petersburg, Richmond could not last long.

Lee and Grant both knew the importance of Petersburg. In Grant's original plan for 1864, he had ordered the small army under Butler to attack it, though Beauregard had successfully defended it. Knowing that the campaign was headed toward Petersburg was one reason why Lee felt the intense need to seize the initiative from Grant and fight him somewhere, anywhere, north of Richmond. As he said to Jubal Early, "We must destroy this army of Grant's before he gets to the James

River. If he gets there, it will become a siege, and then it will be a mere question of time." Time was indeed what Lee had on his mind and on his hands as he stared across his trenches at Grant's army.

Grant had begun his assault on Beauregard on June 15, and though Beauregard had not broken Grant had still managed to cut off two of the four rail lines into the city and two of its major roads. Lee arrived in time to save the various routes coming in from the southwest, but serious damage had already been done. Lee could not allow any more if he hoped to hold Richmond. He had foreseen this eventuality, and work on the Petersburg trenches had been ongoing while he fought the Overland Campaign. As a result, when he settled into his positions, his lines were essentially impenetrable. After Cold Harbor, Grant did not dare ask his men for another direct assault, and so he decided on his siege.

To be clear, Petersburg was not a siege in the truest sense of the term. In a real siege, one army surrounds or otherwise cuts another off from all supply or help sufficient to maintain itself. It then simply waits until its opponents get hungry and thirsty enough to give up or break under an assault. The army conducting the seige may try to hasten the end by making life as bad for its enemies as possible through bombardments or other sorts of ranged attacks. If the besieged are willing to give up their position, they can try to break out. If not, they can only hope to hold out long enough for rescue. This is what Grant had done to Vicksburg in 1863. In Lee's case, Grant had not closed him off from supplies, but he had pinned him to a position that he could not afford to leave. Davis was dedicated to holding the capital to the bitter end, and as a result that end proved to be bitter indeed. Grant finally had Lee exactly where he wanted him. Lee could not maneuver, and Grant could pound his army until it came apart.

Petersburg had been the last place Lee had wanted to move his army, and he knew what the inevitable results would be. By that time, though, if he was to do his duty and prevent Grant from winning the war immediately, he had no choice. Not only did Davis demand it, but Lee was now almost completely reliant upon his entrenchments. His army by this point had dwindled to less than 50,000 men and Grant's boasted over 100,000 again and was still growing. Without his trenches Lee stood no real chance of facing Grant in a straight battle.

The siege at Petersburg would last for nine grueling months. All that time, as Grant received regular reinforcements, he lengthened his left flank to the west. Lee had no choice but to stretch his own line to match, and he had to do it with the force that he had on hand. While Grant could fully man his trenches, Lee's lines were gradually pulled thinner and thinner. Grant would periodically test Lee's lines with attacks, knowing that eventually Lee would break somewhere. In Richmond, shortages began to tell as most of the few supplies making it into the city had to be diverted to the army protecting it. Whereas Richmond had once been the pride of the Confederacy, a head of cabbage now cost $10, a quart of milk $2.50, and a bushel of potatoes $160. The hospitals were filled with wounded and sickness was common. Still, the people tried to get on with life as best they could.

The war at this point very much prefigured what the world would see in World War I, with vast, complex trench systems arranged one row after the other. Lee's men huddled down in muddy, filthy ditches while exposed to all kinds of weather. Men froze in the winter, suffered the heat in the summer, and contracted various illnesses year round. At the rare times when the attacks came, they would shoot down their enemies in a bloody rout, and then go back to doing little or nothing. The soldier who described war as "two months of complete boredom punctuated by twenty minutes of sheer terror," may well have been sitting in one of Lee's trenches.

Where Civil War trench fighting can be best distinguished from that of World War I is in the level of technology involved and the amount of murder that took place. By World War I, most soldiers were armed with bolt action rifles fed with clips that allowed a much faster rate of fire. They were supported by machine guns that sprayed the field with hundreds of rounds each minute, and their artillery could be ranged to hit targets a mile away, allowing many guns to be placed in the rear of a line and massive amounts of fire to be laid down on a specific area. The invention of barbed wire meant that armies could quickly and cheaply create multiple barriers to advancement at different points in front of them. The result was slaughter on such a scale that an entire generation of Europeans was wiped out in only a few years of fighting. In 1864, though some rapid fire weapons had begun to appear, most soldiers were armed with muzzle-loading rifles and backed up by artillery that required crews see their target in order to hit it. They also had no easy way to create serious impediments to their advancing enemies, though they improvised tangles of wooden spikes and logs called abatis. They would set these at the farthest practical range of their rifles and when the enemy had to slow down to get by them, they would open fire. This level of technology obviously resulted in a dramatically slowed rate of fire over what would later come (only one to three rounds per minute per soldier in 1864), and their artillery placement was limited by necessity. The abatis worked, but could usually be passed in a serious attack. Even so, Civil War soldiers still dealt out plenty of death, as Cold Harbor demonstrated. All of the principles that would make World War I so vicious were present with Lee at Petersburg.

Lee's most significant attempt to relieve the siege had begun before it had technically started. As the armies sat at Cold Harbor, Lee created the Army of the Valley out of the Second Corps of the Army of Northern Virginia and he placed Early in charge. Lee wanted Early to invade the Shenandoah and perhaps threaten Washington, D.C. in the hope that it would force Grant to split his own forces in order to defend the capital and therefore relieve some of the pressure on Lee. The move proved well timed, because almost simultaneously, a Union force led by David Hunter was closing in on Lynchburg, Virginia, in Lee's rear. Lynchburg was a small city, but its location had made it a transportation hub. Therefore, many of Lee's scant supplies passed through the city. Grant recognized its importance, and had said that he believed that if they could just take and hold Lynchburg for "one day," it would be a serious blow to Lee's army.

Hunter was an abolitionist general who very much embodied the rhetoric of hard war and tried in varying degrees to act on it. He had begun his raid in the Shenandoah by burning homes and businesses with impunity. As he advanced, he also destroyed the Virginia Military Institute on the grounds that its cadets had often participated in the war. When questioned on it, Hunter replied that he intended to burn the University of Virginia too when he reached it. As Hunter approached Lynchburg from the west, Lee sent Early to defend the city and repel the attack. The two armies met in the "Battle" of Lynchburg on June 17–18, which was really more of a large skirmish. After very little fighting, Hunter, a political general with no real wartime experience, decided to retreat, and retreated so effectively that he took his little army entirely out of the war.

Seeing the opportunity to cause some creative mischief, Lee set Early loose to fulfill his original mission. Early entered the valley and marched north, crossing the Potomac on July 5 and advancing toward Washington. This had its desired effect, and Grant began detaching forces to send to Washington. General Lew Wallace intercepted Early, but was heavily outnumbered. Early defeated Wallace on July 9 in the Battle of Monocacy, but the action had cost him a day. He arrived on the outskirts of Washington just as significant reinforcements came in from the other side. Early skirmished a little but then decided to fall back to Leesburg. By July 16, the Army of the Valley was on its way back to the Shenandoah.

Early's raid had only limited effects. Grant did dispatch forces in response, but he had so many more troops than Lee that it did not even the odds enough for Lee to resume the offensive. Once again, it might be argued that Lee had prolonged the war, but he did so out of duty not hope. By this point, Lee had returned to the original expectation of defeat with which he had started the war, and knew that there would not be much time left. It was his job to fight the war as best he could and he would do so, leaving the rest to God and the politicians.

Grant's most dramatic gamble to end the war early came about in late July as a result of some planning by Ambrose Burnside. After he had lost command of the army he never believed himself fit to lead, Burnside had returned to his corps. There, as before, he had done a solid job as a leader. He was now serving with Grant's army in the trenches around Petersburg. While there, some of his soldiers approached him with a plan to blow up a large section of Lee's line. Several Pennsylvania coal miners were convinced that they could dig a tunnel from inside their lines, all the way under the space between the armies, and end up under the Army of Northern Virginia. Once there, they would dig laterally, creating long galleries that could be packed with explosives. Burnside took the plan to Grant, who was skeptical, but allowed it go ahead.

The miners then made the impossible happen with the help of an ingenious ventilation system of their own design. When complete, their tunnel was 511 feet long. Burnside, an abolitionist, gave special training to a division of black soldiers who were to charge into the gap created in Lee's line and end the war. The Confederates had some indications of what was coming; rumors circulated through the trenches that Burnside had sent a division of African Americans to dig a mine under the Confederates, and that some men had actually heard the digging. This was obviously a conglomeration of the truth sent through the rumor mill, but close enough that they could have avoided what was to come. Lee and the rest of the officers dismissed the intelligence as nonsense from the "scamps in the trenches."

By July 29, Burnside's men were packing the galleries with 8,000 pounds of black powder and they were ready to begin. At that point, everything started going wrong. When Grant realized that Burnside was not only serious about his plan to blow up Confederate lines but also serious about sending in his division of black soldiers, he intervened at the last minute. Grant was worried that if things did not go as planned, he would be wrongly accused of using the colored troops as cannon fodder. He ordered Burnside to substitute a white division that had not been trained in the special assault tactics needed. Burnside had no choice but to do so.

The resulting explosion on the morning of July 30 ripped a giant gash in the earth roughly 200 feet long, 70 feet wide, and 25 feet deep. The troops on either side who managed to survive the initial blast were buried alive as the tons of dirt and debris thrown into the air tumbled back down on top of them. It opened a long breach in Lee's lines almost 500 feet wide. The replacement division attacked, but did not know what it was doing. Instead of charging around the crater and into the Confederate rear, they ran directly into it. Unable to quickly scale the other side, they became easy targets for the surviving Confederates who rapidly lined the edges. When Lee learned what had happened, he rushed reinforcements to the scene and watched from nearby. Burnside's African American division followed, hoping to salvage the situation, but they only added to the slaughter by providing more targets. After the initial tactical blunder, the result was decided. The Battle of the Crater resulted in 4,400 Federal casualties, while Lee lost 1,500 men, most killed in the initial blast. After the Crater, Grant returned to his policy of extending his line and periodically probing Lee's. He did so without Burnside, whose career was effectively over.

One important result of the Crater was to bring the Army of Northern Virginia into contact with black troops for the first time. Once they got over the shock, the slaughter began. Many African Americans soldiers were killed outright in the battle, and some who were allowed to surrender were summarily executed by various bitter Southerners afterward. Porter Alexander observed that there "was without doubt a great deal of unnecessary killing of them." Lee made no direct mention of the incidents, at least none have survived. It is therefore impossible to know exactly what he knew or what he thought of them. Given how widespread the stories became, it is hard to believe he knew nothing. Whatever the case, he did nothing to punish the offenders or to issue orders against future incidents. It may be that Lee thought this was a battle he could not win with his troops, and therefore remained silent to keep morale high. It may also be that he had come to accept the brutalities of this war as simply a fact of life. Without more evidence, history will not be able to say with any certainty.

The aftermath of the Petersburg Crater, 1865. (Library of Congress.)

Some of the worst pressures on Lee's army during the nine months of siege did not come from Grant's army; they came from news about the rest of the Confederacy. While Davis still dogmatically insisted that they would be winning the war again within a year, even the most casual observer could see that things were falling apart quickly. Out in the Shenandoah, things went well for Early for a time, but after his successes, Grant dispatched Sheridan to deal with him. Sheridan was an aggressive cavalry commander who would pursue the Confederates until he had cleared the valley. Early fenced with Sheridan, but suffered a final defeat at Cedar Creek on October 19. Lee called most of the remaining forces back to Petersburg by December, and Sheridan returned to Grant, his mission accomplished. The Union had finally seized control of the Shenandoah.

Even more distressing, perhaps, was Sherman's progress in Georgia. For a time, Confederates clung to the hope that Lincoln would be voted out of office by a frustrated North in the election of 1864, but when Sherman took Atlanta in September, Lincoln easily beat George McClellan for a second term in office. Worse, while Sherman dispatched enough troops to deal with John Bell Hood's invasion of Tennessee, Sherman himself embarked on his infamous March to the Sea from Atlanta to Savannah. Along the way, he destroyed Georgia's railroad network and used up as many excess supplies as his army could. Sherman arrived in Savannah on December 24, offering the city to Lincoln as a Christmas present.

The previously untouched heartland of Georgia and the lush Shenandoah had been Lee's last two significant areas from which to draw recruits and supplies. With both of them denied to him, his army began to suffer from increasing shortages of all kinds. Worse, as Union troops passed through their homes, soldiers in his ranks began hearing about what was happening. Their families wrote them letters pleading with them to come back and take care of things at home. The thousands of men who had enlisted to protect their families from the Yankee invasion no longer saw a point to the war, and they started deserting by the hundreds. Lee's own frustrations continued to mount as his army disintegrated around him. He reported that his men were becoming more and more undisciplined, and found there was little he could do to change things. In January, he warned Davis that "Grant will be enabled to envelope Richmond, or turn both of our flanks & I see no way of increasing our strength." He saw what was coming, knew what needed to happen in order to prevent the inevitable, but could do nothing other than fight as long as he could.

Early in 1865, the Confederate government finally appointed Lee commander in chief of all their armies. Of course, by this time the act was as pointless as it was desperate. Had Lee ascended to that office earlier, in 1862 perhaps or even 1863, there might have been a very different course to the Civil War. As it stood, Lee was appointed only when events were too far advanced for him to do much of anything. He appointed Johnston to command what little remained of the Army of Tennessee after Hood wrecked it outside Nashville. Lee then sent Johnston to oppose Sherman, who was beginning his advance north through the Carolinas, using them up much as he had Georgia. Johnston was as badly outnumbered as Lee and could do little more than slow Sherman's march. Eventually, Sherman would reach Grant and the two would combine to form an army so large it could break the Confederates at will.

Lee probably decided to act one more time rather than wait for the death blow. After conferring with Davis, he ordered Gordon to organize an assault on Ft. Stedman, on the far left of his line. On the morning of March 25, Gordon's men launched a brilliant surprise attack that captured the fort with almost no Confederate casualties. After that, though, the plan fell apart. What the scouts had identified as Federal forts and the next points of attack turned out to be old, empty Confederate works. Gordon's men blundered about trying to find their way, and a Union counterattack crushed them, sending them reeling back into their own lines.

The end Lee had foreseen came on quickly once it began. Lee hoped to punch his way through the Union line in preparation for linking up with Johnston's army in North Carolina. He then might have a ghost of a chance of defeating Grant and Sherman in detail. It was an unlikely ploy, but there really was little left to try. Pickett's men attacked at Five Forks on the right, and made some initial progress. Unfortunately, Sheridan struck back on April 1, shattering Pickett's forces. Lee tried to recover his line, but on April 2 Grant ordered a general attack along the front. Another tragedy befell Lee in the early dawn that day when A. P. Hill rode out to try to find out what was going on. He and a courier encountered a line of Federal skirmishers and tried to bluff their way out of the situation by demanding that they surrender. The Union soldiers responded by opening fire, shooting Hill through the heart. He was knocked from the saddle and died before he hit the ground. "He is at rest now," Lee said, "and we who are left are the ones to suffer." Of the once mighty leadership of the Army of Northern Virginia, Lee now had only Longstreet left with him.

With Federal soldiers pouring through his lines at several points, Lee sent word to Davis that he could not hold, and that Richmond would shortly fall. The capital was thrown into utter confusion as the government and its citizens attempted to flee before Lee's army retreated. That night, Lee abandoned Petersburg and fled west, hoping to get around Grant's flank and make it to Danville. From there, Lee could use the trains to reach Johnston, his last hope. At this point, Lee well knew that such a scheme was a practical impossibility, but as a soldier it was his duty to fight as long as he could unless ordered to surrender by Davis, something that even now Davis would not countenance.

Lee hoped that Federal forces would be delayed in their pursuit and then that they would not press him hard. This was unrealistic, even given that the Union must occupy both Petersburg and Richmond and the fact that Meade—who was still technically in command of the Army of the Potomac, at least—had moved slowly in pursuit after Gettysburg. Grant was there, and he would not let Lee escape if he could. By the evening of April 3, however, Lee was 21 miles away from Petersburg, once more in open territory and able to maneuver against Grant. His disparate troops began to report in, and things seemed to have improved somewhat.

The Army of Northern Virginia successfully reached Amelia Courthouse on April 4, where Lee expected to find provisions for his army. Upon arrival, they found nothing—no food or ammunition. An enraged Lee could do nothing but halt his army for the day and send it out to forage for supplies. While they did, Lee scrambled to order more supplies sent to him from Lynchburg and Danville. His foraging parties found very little food, and he had wasted a precious 24 hours of his lead over Grant. Lee himself said that the delay was "fatal, and could not be retrieved."

Lee resumed the march on April 5, trying to make up for the lost time with an exhausted, famished army that continued to shrink by the hour. About one o'clock that afternoon, Lee met his first serious check: Sheridan's cavalry, backed up by infantry, had blocked the road ahead of them and the Federals were entrenching madly. Though Lee's instincts told him to attack, he decided it would be futile and instead turned toward Farmville, where 80,000 rations awaited him. The army marched all night in a desperate attempt to reach them before the Federals.

On the morning of the 6th, another disaster struck Lee's army. In the confusion brought on by the exhausting marches, part of a wagon train had mixed in with Longstreet's command. Its tired mules could hardly pull their burdens, and so they slowly fell behind, separating one half of Longstreet's command from the other. That afternoon, Federal cavalry found the stragglers at Sayler's Creek and the horsemen were soon joined by the Sixth Corps of the Army of the Potomac. They smashed the Confederates completely. Though Lee sent reinforcements, in that one engagement he lost a quarter of the small army he had left to him. "My God!" Lee lamented when he saw the scene, "Has the army been dissolved?" Lee had lost roughly 8,000 men, and both his son Custis and Ewell, one of his few remaining corps commanders, had been captured. Successive defeats had reduced the once mighty Army of Northern Virginia to a scant 15,000 men, including 3,000 cavalry. Chasing them, Grant could call on at least 80,000.

Lee reached Farmville before Grant's men and found his provisions, but he could not stop for long. By dark on April 7, the remnant of his army had already pushed on. Grant kept pressing, forcing Lee to periodically deploy his men to keep the Federals at bay. That evening, a Federal courier under a flag of truce found Lee. He carried a note from Grant. Grant stated that the battles of the last week had made it clear that there could be no more effective resistance. He asked Lee to consider the surrender of his army to avoid any more useless death. Lee consulted Longstreet, who was there. Longstreet simply replied, "Not yet." Lee sent word to Grant that he had read the note and though he still thought his army capable of effective resistance, he would like to know Grant's terms of surrender. Grant replied that he would insist that the men and officers of the army lay down their arms and agree to abide by their paroles until they had been formally exchanged. Lee offered to discuss the broader surrender of the Confederate armies under his command in the hopes of bringing peace sooner. He proposed they meet at 10 o'clock the next morning on the Old Stage Road from Richmond, between the two armies.

While this was going on, Lee tried to keep his army together and keep it moving. On April 8, Lee dismissed a sizable representation of his few remaining commanders, including Pickett and corps commander Anderson. Lee had been disgusted with their performance since Five Forks, and as long as he commanded his army, he would discipline it to the best of his ability. He also deflected pointed suggestions of surrender from some of his other subordinates, including artillery officer William Pendleton. Even as he was actively negotiating with Grant, he refused to have his men talk of surrender and did not inform them that he was considering it.

As Lee moved on to Appomattox, he received news that Sheridan's cavalry had once again beaten him. Sheridan had managed to circle around the entire army and get in front of Lee. Lee's own cavalry had discovered them entrenching. That night, in addition to writing Grant, Lee held a last council of war with his remaining commanders. At this point, that included Longstreet, Gordon, and Fitz Lee of the cavalry. The answer they arrived at was simple: They must attack or surrender. Lee ordered Gordon to attack at dawn, and then retired for a few hours of sleep.

Early the next morning, April 9, Lee rose and dressed in his best uniform, featuring a fine red silk sash and sword. Lee normally avoided shows of what he thought were pretension, but he evidently believed that the occasion would warrant it. Lee then left to follow the progress of Gordon's attack. When he arrived, he could not see much of the fighting and about 8:00 A.M. he sent one of his staff ahead to find out what was happening. Lee learned that Gordon's attack had at first been successful and they had pressed Sheridan's cavalry back. Unfortunately, before they achieved any decisive results, a strong force of Union infantry had arrived. Overwhelmed, Gordon had to withdraw or face being cut off from Longstreet. Gordon sent Lee word that he had "fought my corps to a frazzle, and I fear I can do nothing unless I am heavily supported by General Longstreet's corps." Lee responded with finality, "Then there is nothing left for me to do but to go and see General Grant, and I would rather die a thousand deaths."

There was simply nothing more for the Army of Northern Virginia to do, in practical terms. For the families of the men killed since April 2, it would even be legitimate to ask if Lee had been right to continue the retreat as long as he had. By this time, Lee had 10,000 men or less and Grant outnumbered them by a margin of over eight to one. The confederates simply could not sustain a war fought along conventional lines. Pundits at the time and since have argued that Lee could still have dispersed his army and fought a guerilla war against the North. That plan was indeed proposed to Lee by Alexander, but Lee dismissed it. Lee pointed out that the army had no supplies to give the men, they had been demoralized by four years of war, and they had no way to return home. Therefore, if Lee turned them loose on the countryside, it would only increase the bitterness and destruction wreaked by the war. Even if they succeeded in actually doing more damage to the Federals than they did to Southern civilians, they most likely would not change the outcome of the war. In fact, they would make the inevitable reunion much more difficult.

Already, Lee was transforming himself from a merchant of war to one of peace. Now that Lee felt he had done his duty and there was no real hope of victory left, he tried to see to the safety of his men and then to the welfare of the South as a whole. Lee did not know what reunion would mean, but in theory it could be anything from a relatively smooth process to a difficult one where a vindictive North sought to impose its will on the South at all costs. Lee was already doing what he could to avoid the latter, and he advised others to follow his example.

Grant did not meet Lee at the appointed time that morning. Instead, he sent a messenger to say that he did not have the authority to arrange for a broader peace, since that power lay with the president. He did want to come to terms with Lee and his army soon, preferably without the loss of another life. As Lee was dictating his response, a rider from Longstreet arrived with news that another possible route of escape had been found. Lee, however, decided the time had come, and let the last route go untraveled. He returned to his letter to Grant. "I now request an interview in accordance with the offer contained in your letter of yesterday for [the purpose of surrendering the army]." Lee suggested a suspension of hostilities until the matter had been decided. A few tense moments followed, as orders for a Federal advance had already been given and no one could find Grant. At the last moment, Meade stepped in and countermanded the attack, preventing a blood bath.

After three hours of waiting, Grant's response finally came. He was coming to the front as quickly as he could to see Lee, and asked where Lee wanted to meet. They settled on the house of Wilmer McLean. McLean had formerly resided around Manassas Junction, and he and his family had been present for the First Battle of Bull Run, where a cannonball had unceremoniously intruded on the privacy of his kitchen. When the armies returned for a second round in 1862, McLean had moved his family to Appomattox Courthouse, where he expected to be able to sit out the rest of the war in peace. This led to McLean being able to say ironically—while having to stretch the truth only a little—that the "war began in my front yard and ended in my front parlour."

Lee rode to the house and waited for Grant. The latter arrived about a half an hour later. Grant was splattered with mud, unbuttoned, in his usual private's uniform, and made a stark contrast to the impeccable dress of Lee. They made some small talk about their mutual experiences in the Mexican War before Lee suggested that they get down to the business at hand. Grant sat down and wrote out the terms of surrender. His terms were generous, though Lee asked for a few modifications. In particular, Lee pointed out that in the Confederate armies the horses were privately owned, and if the men were to be able to grow food for their families the next year, they would need to keep them. Grant agreed. In the end, all of the army's offensive equipment—rifles, cannon, and so forth—were to be turned over to Grant's men. The Confederate officers could keep their private side arms and horses. Any other soldiers who wanted to could claim a horse as well. They must immediately return home and not take up arms against the United States again. As long as they abided by the terms of their parole, Grant guaranteed that they would go unmolested by the United States government. He went a step further to order that 25,000 rations be sent over to the hungry Confederates.

Lee shook Grant's hand and bowed to everyone in the room. He then walked outside and called for Traveller. While he looked out over the landscape, he drove his fist into his hand three times, and then mounted when Traveller arrived. He must face one more difficult duty that day: He had to break the news to his men. For them the long war was finally over. It was now time to learn how to face peace with the very nation they had spent four years trying to destroy. Grant came out onto the porch as Lee began to ride away. Both generals saluted each other once more and Lee left the McLean property.

Grant maintained a respectable calm and betrayed no signs of joy or exultation at having finally bested Lee. When word of the surrender made its way out into the Union army, loud celebrations began immediately. The cheers could be heard for miles and even normally staid, sour generals like Meade joined in. Grant quickly put a stop to it. Lee and his army had surrendered honorably and Grant did not want his men to mock them at the culmination of their long, hard-fought defeat. They were to be treated as the soldiers they were.

Back at the McLean house, a rather comical scene ensued. A number of Federals, conscious of the historic event they had just witnessed, determined to get their own piece of it. McLean soon found himself having to bargain for nearly every item in the surrender room. Sheridan started it off with an offer for 20 dollars in gold for the table Lee used to sign the surrender. From there, officers wheedled and bargained their way through the whole room, leaving it completely empty. The only items that were not purchased were the smaller ones soldiers simply took and walked off with without paying for them at all. This sort of gold digging for history was taken to an extreme much later when the property was sold to speculators in 1891. They actually took the house entirely apart and planned to reassemble it at the 1893 Chicago World's Fair. The plan fell through due to money problems and the building sat in storage for years. It was finally successfully reassembled on the original property in stages in the 1940s.

Virtually all that was left of the army had gathered close to Lee's headquarters, and as he rode by they cheered him loudly. Even in their dire position, he was still their invincible leader. Something in Lee's face was different this time, though, and the cheers slowly died away. The reality of surrender had begun to dawn on the Army of Northern Virginia and as it became clearer what had happened, many openly wept. Some of them spoke while Lee passed, others just reached out and touched Traveller's side. Lee had never been very good at speeches, but he did a better job now, when opportunity presented itself. "Boys," he said, "I have done the best I can for you. Go home now and if you make as good citizens as you have soldiers, you will do well and I shall be proud of you. Goodbye and God bless you all." Lee went inside his tent, and the men slowly drifted away.

Lee retired to an apple orchard in order to remain available and there he faced the first hours after his defeat alone. His staff officers described him as being in one of his "savage moods" and they tried to stay away from him and encouraged others to do the same. Swarms of Federal soldiers roamed through the Confederate camps, some looking for friends, some hunting mementos, and others just exploring. Many of them came by the grove trees to observe Lee, though Lee's staff officers kept back all but the most important visitors. Lee paced back and forth as he tried to come to grips with what had happened and that, when taken with the crowds of gawkers kept back at a safe distance, led more than one witness and biographer to liken Lee to a great cat at some zoo. Lee was coldly cordial with anyone distinguished enough to make it through the cordon, and he made sure to see to all of the surrender responsibilities.

The war had indeed been terrible. Over 600,000 Americans had been killed and perhaps more than a million more had been wounded, maimed, or injured. Though it is hard to accurately estimate the number of Confederate casualties, the South may well have lost approximately the same number of soldiers as the North and that number came from a much smaller population. Very few Southern homes had escaped some sort of personal loss during the war. Most of the South's largest cities had been occupied and much of what little industrial base they had enjoyed previous to the war had been wrecked. Complicating matters even more, millions of former slaves had gained their freedom but they had little else. With no money, no land, and no hope of getting any, they were as doomed to poverty as their former white masters who had lost their wealth, labor, and many of their tangible assets.

Lee himself was now homeless, as Mary's precious Arlington had already become a cemetery for Union dead and would never be returned to them. Over the course of the war, he had lost his daughter, his daughter-in-law, and two of his grandchildren. Mary's rheumatism had advanced to the point where she was essentially an invalid, and Lee had ruined his own health through the strain of campaigning. Indeed, had the war not ended when it did, Lee may not have survived the stress and strain much longer. He had also destroyed his career of service, turning traitor to the country he had served for so long.

The good news of Appomattox was that Grant's conduct of the surrender did much to help smooth the process of national reunification, even if it did not stamp out all remnants of Confederate sympathy. The fact that he treated Lee and his soldiers both generously and honorably defused what could have potentially been an explosive situation. The famous Chinese commander Sun Tzu remarked in his *Art of War* that it is never wise to completely cut off an enemy from escape, because that would force him to fight to the last, drawing out the war, breeding hatred for occupying forces, and costing a commander dearly. Grant unknowingly followed this advice. He had left the Army of Northern Virginia an open door to end the war honorably, and the exhausted Confederates had taken advantage of it.

That night, Lee delegated the writing of his farewell orders to Charles Marshall, though Lee himself undoubtedly oversaw their basic content. Marshall praised the men's devotion and courage, but stated that there had been no further hope of continuing the war in light of massive Union superiority in men and material. They were, he said, free to return to their homes until officially exchanged. Of course, by this point, no one expected any exchanges to happen. Before long the war would be over everywhere and already the Confederacy was a dead letter in all but the most ardent Rebel's dreams. Others would go on fighting, but more because they wanted to contend for the title of "last to surrender" than in hope of victory. Lee tidied up the last few details of the process, secured his own parole according to the terms Grant had generously offered, and finally left for Richmond on April 12, after his army had finally dispersed.

Chapter 8

CONCILIATION, DIPLOMACY, AND IDOLIZATION

The Robert Edward Lee that rode into Richmond in 1865 was a very different man than the one who had arrived there in 1861 and the city he found had become a very different place. Quite a bit of it had been burned in the evacuation when Lee's lines had finally broken less than a month before. He made his way to 707 Franklin Street, the last in the string of homes his family had occupied during the war. He had not seen his loved ones much during the past four years, and now he must get to know them all over again. In many ways, it would have been like meeting them for the first time. When Lee arrived at the house, he passed quietly inside, pausing only to bow to the people who had assembled outside.

Lee spent much of his time over the next few weeks sleeping, trying to recover from the extreme stress and strain of four years of war. Once people knew that Lee was in the city, a steady stream of visitors began to call on him for any and all reasons, but particularly to get the chance to simply observe Lee and talk to him. His sons took turns manning the door, turning away almost everyone. If Lee were awake, he would often receive anyone who came by kindly, in spite of his sons' efforts. Still, Lee did not enjoy the fame he had achieved. When he started feeling better, he had to begin taking his walks at night just to avoid gawkers and onlookers. Some of those who came by did have legitimate business and even did history a great service by leaving records of their visits, such as when photographer Matthew Brady arrived and convinced Lee and his sons to sit for one of the few pictures taken of him at the time.

Lee wanted to get out of Richmond and away from all of the attention, but had no clear idea of how to do it. He had never owned a home himself, and had instead lived primarily on Mary's interest in Arlington. With Arlington lost, he had no place to go. His sons still owned some of the Custis estates they had inherited, but he showed no desire to move in with them. He would be able to recover some of the money he had scrupulously saved before the war, but not as much as he would need to realize his dream of buying a small, pleasant farm and settling down in the country. He also had no other real source of income with which to supplement his savings.

Matthew Brady's photograph of Lee, taken not long after Appomattox. (Library of Congress.)

For a while, too, there was an open question as to whether Lee would even be free to pursue his idyllic dreams at all. He had, after all, been one of the most effective generals in a massive rebellion against government authority that had resulted in the deaths of hundreds of thousands of men. Traditionally, victorious governments had taken men like Lee, put them on trial, and then either imprisoned them or had them hanged. After President Davis had been captured in Georgia and thrown in prison, there was some talk of also arresting Lee. Lee believed himself to be protected by the terms of the surrender to Grant, which stated that as long as soldiers abided by the terms of their parole, they would be protected from prosecution and government harassment. Of course, the war was over and so Lee was technically no longer a prisoner of war on parole. When the talk of arresting Lee was loudest, Lee wrote to Grant to remind him of their agreement and ask for his help. Grant, who saw the threat to Lee as an issue of personal honor, took the question up with President Andrew Johnson himself and ensured that Lee would never face trial.

Of course, that did not mean that life as a United States citizen would go on as usual for Lee. Lee believed very much that the South's best hope now was to try to reintegrate into the political process and defend its rights at the ballot box. To that end, he encouraged everyone to whom he spoke on the matter to abide by the laws and rules that the North enforced and to accept the new order of things, hoping to preserve as much as possible of what they loved about the old Union. Lee himself took the oath of allegiance in October and applied for a pardon from the president. His appeal fell on deaf ears. In fact, Secretary of State William Seward gave the signed oath to a friend as a keepsake rather than pass it along through official channels. Along with other high ranking Confederate generals and statesmen, Lee was never granted his rights as a citizen, though he was also never bothered by the government. Lee was only granted citizenship status 110 years later in 1975 by President Gerald Ford when his lost appeal finally resurfaced.

As the years passed, Lee continued to defy the modern stereotypes of racial expectations, at times making statements that were blatantly racist, but then doing things that even some contemporary abolitionists would hesitate to do. During his time in Richmond and later, Lee regularly expressed his opinion that the former slaves were inferior to whites and he thought they tended to be shortsighted and lazy. On one occasion when he gave testimony before Congress, he stated that he believed Virginia would be better off when its black population had migrated elsewhere. That would seem to imply that he had become hardened in explicitly racist views. On the other hand, while the Lee family was attending church in Richmond one Sunday, a well-dressed black man had the audacity to walk forward to the church's altar when the call for communion was issued. There was dead silence for a moment as the embarrassed rector stood in front of the kneeling supplicant, the congregation shifting in their seats uncomfortably. Then Lee himself stood up and walked down the aisle. He knelt next to the man, treating him as every bit his own spiritual equal.

Lee left Richmond with what remained of his family on June 28, 1865, and moved to Derwent, a small house in a grove of old oaks owned by Elizabeth Cocke. Cocke allowed the Lees to live there rent

Lee's family residence in Richmond, Virginia. (Library of Congress.)

free, and they passed a pleasant but stuffy summer, trying to decide what to do next. A number of lucrative (and sometimes sketchy) business proposals poured in from across the country, and virtually every one of them was primarily concerned with securing Lee's name more than Lee himself. Lee turned down every scheme presented to him until one finally caught his attention: He had been voted in as president of Washington College in Lexington, Virginia.

Washington College was a small, struggling school that had begun years before as Liberty Hall Academy. Situated as it was in Lexington, it was a neighbor of the Virginia Military Institute, where "Stonewall" Jackson had once taught. The college had suffered as a result of the war, especially after David Hunter's men had ransacked it in 1864 before burning VMI, and the generally poor state of the Southern economy had left it without much money. At the time the board met in the summer of 1865 to consider a new president, only four professors and very few students remained.

Feeling that they could benefit from Lee's patronage—as did many others—the board of trustees had voted Lee in as president and only then got around to consulting him. They sent Judge John W. Brockenbrough to Derwent to inform Lee and offer him the position. Lee would be expected to oversee the operations of the college and to teach one class, which had generally been in philosophy. Lee would, of course, also be expected to lend his considerable reputation to fundraising efforts. In exchange, Lee would receive a salary of $1,500 a year, a house with a garden, and 20 percent of all tuition paid by the students. Brockenbrough also emphasized that Lee would be working to rebuild the South and improve its future by improving its young men, the very people who would be responsible for resurrecting their section.

Lee thought about the offer for two weeks before accepting. He did insist that he be relieved of teaching duties, since he did not feel that he was gifted in that area and was worried about his health. He also insisted that the board consider his appointment carefully. He had of course become more than aware of the fact that as many people across the country now cursed as praised him, and he did not want his connection to the school to hurt it in any way. The board quickly agreed to Lee's conditions and assured him that they were proud to have him as their president. They also immediately began fundraising.

Lee's reasons for moving back into academia were probably at least twofold. First, even though he could probably have successfully put himself forward for a more prestigious position at a larger school, Lee was still to some extent an idealist. He really did want to make a difference in the education of the South, which was experiencing a crisis at that point, and Washington College would give him a freer hand than other, more established schools. Second, the simple fact was that Lee needed money and a place to live. With his military career obviously over, he had no income and apart from his scant savings he and his family were living entirely on someone else's charity. For a man like Lee, that was a difficult burden to bear. His position as president would allow him to aid the South in the way he thought best and at the same time provide for his family.

The whole situation was, of course, another irony for Lee. Up to this point in his life, Lee had done everything he possibly could to avoid being dragged into education. He had disliked his time as an instructor at West Point and had (politely) tried to get out of his assignment there later as superintendent. He had simply never believed that he was much good at education. Here, however, Lee saw a chance to make a difference.

When Washington College approached Lee initially, they may simply have been looking for a convenient "Hero in Residence" whose name they could make use of, but they got much more. Lee was very determined to enhance the education of the students there and over time he made significant improvements. To their credit, the board worked with him easily. Lee obtained money for the school from many sources, including $10,000 from Cyrus McCormick, inventor of the mechanical reaper. Paid agents scoured the country, bringing the college's funding back up to a respectable level. Lee used the money to transform the curriculum of the school from a traditional classical approach that emphasized great works and ancient languages to what amounted to a modern university. Lee placed a much stronger emphasis on the hard sciences, such as physics and engineering, and he gave the students much more of a choice in what they studied. This allowed them to prepare for multiple careers depending on their own likes, needs, and interests.

Lee also began a significant upgrade of the buildings on campus, starting with his own house. The campus in general had been neglected both during and before the war, and Lee now had to put it back in order. The president's house had actually been rented out to a doctor in town and so restoration work could not begin until after his lease had ended. Until then, Lee lived in a rented room and his family stayed with friends. When renovations did get underway, Lee had to personally schedule and oversee all of the work himself. Though he seemed to enjoy it, the process proved so time consuming that he asked the college board to appoint someone else to take care of things for him. His family arrived by December 2, and at the end of his first year (1865–1866), there were marked changes at Washington College.

Lee also affected enrollment at the college. After he assumed the presidency, its enrollment jumped from 47 to nearly 150 in one year. He took his role as an educator seriously and played a very personal role in the lives of many of his students. He kept an eye on them in class and in town, and would often write their parents updates on their problems and progress. Becoming very much a father figure for them, he affectionately referred to them as "my boys." He strove to be patient with them when they went astray and do what he could to set them right. That said Lee was not an indulgent parent. The students respected him and at times merely a disapproving look would be all that was necessary to bring about a reformation. For those who did not reform, Lee simply expelled them from the school or allowed them to quietly withdraw.

Lee tried to set a strong example for the students under his care, and his views on education were definitely progressive for his time. He saw the students as somewhere between boys and men and tried to provide enough structure for them that they would not go to foolish excesses while at the same time giving them freedom to make their own choices. Lee also did what he could to allow them the chance to learn from their mistakes and to redeem them rather than setting everything right himself. If they could not or would not, he sent them away rather than tolerate repeated or intentional failure.

As time passed, the United States Congress grew more and more frustrated with the intransigence it saw exhibited in the South. It became increasingly clear that most white Southerners thought the goal of Reconstruction was simply to put things back to where they had been before the war. America had really become a different nation, though, and the victorious North would not tolerate just a return to what had been. There was now a real dedication to seeing the country become a modern, industrialized state and African Americans treated as full citizens. Also, the question of whether or not America was truly one nation under a powerful central government or simply a collection of individual states working together when convenient had been settled. As more and more states reorganized themselves under the less harsh Reconstruction plan Lincoln had advocated and Johnson had implemented, it became increasingly clear that very little had changed in the South. In fact, the same politicians began arriving in Washington that had left it in 1860 and 1861, and former Confederate generals were becoming governors. "Black Codes" were used to relegate former slaves to permanent status as inferiors and to ensure the continued dominance of white Democrats. It was clear that military defeat had so far only brought about the acceptance that the North was more powerful, not that its ideals were right.

The radical Republicans in Congress reacted to this in 1867 by pushing through legislation over Johnson's veto designed to punish the South and force it to accept a new way of thinking. They refused to accept any states reorganized under Johnson's plan and instead demanded that the South bar all former Confederates from government and accept full black equality by formally approving the Thirteenth and Fourteenth Amendments to the Constitution. Until that happened, the Republicans insisted that the states did not actually exist. They were simply various districts under the direct control of the United States Army.

At Lexington, Lee received hundreds of letters asking for help and advice, many of which he answered himself. His response to questions about Reconstruction was consistent: people should scrupulously obey the laws and those who gained the right to vote should exercise it regularly and with care. For Lee, whatever his opinions, the war had decided the questions at hand. He had lost, and therefore would abide by the decision of the battlefield.

Lee's time at Washington College was not without incident, and his status did indeed bring with it trials in addition to benefits. Some

A print showing Robert E. Lee and 21 Confederate generals, published circa 1867. (Library of Congress.)

of these came as a result of the controversies around Reconstruction. A prime example involved the case of a Union veteran, Erastus C. Johnston. Johnston had moved to Lexington in 1865 to begin work with freed slaves. He later opened a store where he lived as well as worked. In January 1868 Johnston had gone skating on the frozen North River. While he had tried to avoid conflict with the various citizens he encountered, a group of youths started harassing and threatening him. Johnston pulled a gun and warned them off, but they attacked him with stones, sticks, and ice. He eventually escaped and made it safely home. Later that night some men arrived at Johnston's store and began beating on the shuttered doors and windows, promising to kill him. Johnston recognized some of them as students at Washington College.

The next morning, Johnston went to the mayor to complain that he felt his life was being threatened. The mayor asked him to explain precisely who did what to whom and Johnston left, convinced that the town was conspiring against him. He then took his case to military authorities and insisted that it be investigated, convinced that everyone involved was somehow connected to Lee's school. Two officers looked into the matter along with Lee himself, and the boys involved were either expelled or allowed to withdraw. This did not satisfy Johnston. He began a letter writing campaign attacking Washington College in newspapers throughout the North. This ballooned into a significant incident as a number of pundits attacked the school on the grounds that it had hired as president a man who had broken his oath to his country and led the Rebel army against it. Worse, the scandal broke just as a major fundraising effort got under way in New York City. Over time, the incident was forgotten and the college began to bring in money again.

Lee's family did not fare as well as his college. Mary continued her steady decline in health, and she and Lee often made trips to the various springs and spas in the area to relax. Any benefits would be temporary, though, and their age continued to tell on them. Lee's children seemed to languish in his very potent shadow. His sons began various sorts of work. Some tried farming, but did not like it much, especially in postwar conditions. Rooney Lee married again and started a family, but Custis took a position at VMI and showed no disposition to sire a flock of his own. He continued to live with his parents and eat at their table. Even Rooney, who was more independent, dutifully submitted his business dealings to his father for approval. Much to their own sorrow, none of Lee's daughters ever married. According to their own accounts, they simply could not find husbands who could measure up to the considerable standard of manhood they had come to expect by observing their father.

One thing that remained a constant in Robert Lee's life was his flirtatious correspondence with younger women. Though once again there is no legitimate reason to suspect Lee of actual impropriety, he continued to keep up his string of letters with pretty girls, many now much, much younger than himself. Even as late as 1869, he was, as one historian put it, "courting" Charlotte Haxall, a beautiful young girl who eventually married his son Rob. While "courting" may be too strong a word, he still demonstrated a gift for complimenting ladies.

Unfortunately, Lee's own health was still in slow but steady decline. His heart continued to pain him and he was increasingly short of breath.

By the winter of 1869, Lee found it difficult to walk the distance from the president's house to the college, though he still enjoyed lengthy rides on his faithful Traveller. His family had a tendency to die young and Lee, though only 63, had begun to look like an old man. His body ached and he moved slowly. Ever the dedicated worker, Lee refused to retire or even to take a vacation, though he admitted that "he felt that he might at any moment die." It was becoming apparent to everyone, especially Lee's doctors, that he needed rest and a chance to get away from his responsibilities. The faculty of Washington College passed a resolution asking Lee to travel farther south to escape the biting cold. His doctors also insisted on the trip, and Lee was finally swayed.

Lee left Lexington with his daughter Agnes on March 24, 1870, on a trip to Savannah, Georgia. Agnes wanted to see the city and Lee wanted to visit his daughter Annie's grave before he died. They took their time, and Agnes was impressed with the people's adulation of her father. In most cities the crowds turned out to pay him respect. In Augusta, Georgia, 13-year-old Woodrow Wilson managed to get close enough to look Lee in the face, something the future president never forgot. Lee was less impressed with the crowds, seeking to avoid the extra attention when possible. He did manage to finally visit his father's grave on the return journey, something that he had wanted to do for decades and which must have brought back an entire lifetime of memories. Though almost constantly harried by visitors, Lee managed to rest and when they finally returned to Lexington on May 26, he was at least no worse than he had been when he left. Given that his vacation had turned into something like a celebrity tour, he could be thankful for that.

Lee did not rest during the summer of 1870. Instead, he embarked on another tour, this time sparked by a visit to a specialist in Baltimore. The doctor, not surprisingly, completely misdiagnosed Lee's condition as simply "rheumatic" and prescribed lemon juice. Lee then visited family in Virginia before returning home at the end of July only to leave again to try out a spa that he had been told had promising cures. Nothing came of his trip there beyond him feeling weaker than before, and he returned to Lexington again.

As the fall came to Lexington, Lee prepared to resume his routine at the college, but he did not feel much stronger than before. He knew that old age was finally overcoming him and he seemed to have been preparing for death for some time. In a real sense, his tours had been as much about taking care of unfinished business as anything else. He had visited the graves of "Light Horse Harry" and his dear Annie, spent time with his living children, and seen as many relatives as he could. When death came, though, it was still surprising.

On September 27, 1870, Lee stepped out into a cold rain to attend a vestry meeting at his local church. He did not particularly want to go, but felt it necessary. The church was discussing expansion plans, and the meeting, which began at 4:00 p.m., ran for three hours. When Lee arrived back home, he went to his room to take off his wet cape and then came down to the dining room. Mary chided him for being late and waited for him to say the grace for the meal. Lee simply stood there, having somehow lost the ability to speak. He seemed to be trying, but was simply unable to force his body to respond to his commands. He sat down and tried to speak again, but still could not. He then straightened up, as if at attention, and it seemed to his family that he knew his time had come.

The family scrambled to help him and put him to bed where he slept quietly for some time while the doctors were called. Lee lingered for two weeks, passing in and out of consciousness. Though Mary felt that he recognized her, he spoke no coherent words, and on most days said nothing at all. Some members of the family remembered the horrible silence for years afterward and the tears they shed as he slowly grew worse. Finally, on October 9, 1870, Lee quietly passed away. Allegedly, his last understandable words were an order to "strike the tent!" He had given those orders hundreds of times before, when moving his headquarters from one place to another. Whether he understood what he was saying or not then, the deeply religious Lee seemed to know he was advancing from one world to the next.

In all likelihood, Lee died as a result of a stroke and the well-intentioned ministrations that followed it. To historians diagnosing his case through the fog of history, it seems that he most likely suffered a loss of blood to his brain (possibly caused by his heart problems) that injured the parts that controlled speech and movement, and, worse, his ability to expectorate. When his attendants poured food, drink, and medicines down his throat, some or all of them ended up in his lungs and he had no way to tell them what they were doing or to cough up the liquids. Pneumonia set in, and at that point he had no hope of recovery.

Lee's story does not end here, however. When Lee left Richmond to move to Lexington, he had a strong, though somewhat localized, reputation. He was known and respected in most areas of the South, but there were many other Confederate heroes—Johnston, Beauregard, and Jackson to name only a few—all jockeying for position directly, though various champions, or a combination thereof. Lee was one of the more prominent Virginia representatives, but for many in the South, Virginia was not the focal point of the war. In Georgia, for instance, they were much more familiar with Johnston, and even in Virginia, Lee shared his fame with Jackson and others.

In the wake of his death, though, Lee's memory became a force all its own, almost completely independent from anything Lee himself had been. Lee was an admirable human being; the followers of what historians have called the "Lee cult" made him into an almost invincible demigod. Lee was transformed from simply an intelligent, largely successful general into a man who not only never lost a battle, but was the very essence of what it meant to be Southern and Confederate. By the time they were through, Lee would hardly have recognized himself if he had read their books and heard their speeches.

The process began, not surprisingly, at Washington College, where Lee's name was immediately used for further fundraising purposes. The trustees and administration walked a fine line, trying to generate money for the college while at the same time paying respect to the legacy of a man they truly admired. Initially they wanted to construct a memorial and crypt for Lee and so they set about raising money. They faced almost immediate competition from another group of Lee enthusiasts who mounted a campaign to build the crypt and memorial in Richmond. After an incredible amount of negotiation and diplomacy, the two factions struck a bargain where Lexington would keep Lee's remains, while Richmond would get his giant equestrian statue.

Part of this compromise provides a good example of how Lee's memory had begun to take on pseudo-religious proportions. Lee Chapel, built in 1867 at Lee's instigation, initially offered regular worship services that Lee himself attended, coming up the stairs from his office in the basement. Later, as the beatification of Lee began, an addition was added to provide for a family crypt to house the bones of Lee and his family below (his mother, father, Mary, and all the children were moved there) and above space was opened for the incredible recumbent statue of Lee, set at the back of the chapel. The effect is striking. When entering the chapel through the back, the viewer is confronted with a more or less standard church scene, with pews facing a raised platform for a speaker. However, instead of a cross or other religious symbol, the area behind the speaker's place is dominated by the statue of Lee. While of course no one actually intends Lee to be worshipped, the effect is obvious. The passion some of Lee's defenders have exhibited (and still do) is easily equal to that of the most enthusiastic of religious believers. For some, the lines between man, myth, and religion became significantly blurred.

This "Lee cult," led by men like former Army of Northern Virginia division and corps commander Jubal Early and early Lee historian J. William Jones, set about placing Lee's claim to military perfection beyond all doubt. In order to do this, of course, they had to find a reason to explain all of Lee's very real failures, something that Lee himself had never shown much interest in. One of their primary routes of attack was the reinvigorated Southern Historical Society and its associated Papers. They set about promoting Virginia as the central theater of the war and Lee as the foremost general in Virginia. To that end, the Lee cult demoted other Confederate commanders and belittled their roles in the conflict in order to promote Lee. For instance, a significant debate broke out between Lee and Jackson supporters over who exactly was responsible for first suggesting the idea of the crushing flank attack that had almost destroyed Hooker's army at Chancellorsville.

Oddly enough, Gettysburg and not Appomattox was what they fought the hardest to explain away. If Lee did not lose Gettysburg, then who did? Perhaps more important, why did it happen that a good cause could be lost? Why had the South been defeated? To sum up the years of wrangling, in response, in only a few pages in any detail is of course impossible, but the best approximation would be to quote historian Thomas Connelly: God and General Longstreet.

Concerning *how* the defeat came about and who was to blame, the Lee cult focused on Longstreet's very real problems at Gettysburg and then magnified them beyond all measure to justify hanging the whole albatross of Confederate defeat around his neck. Longstreet played directly into the hands of his critics by becoming "traitor" to the South and working with the Republican government in Reconstruction. That gave Longstreet a platform from which to speak in the North, but with the Southerners to whom the Lee cult appealed, Longstreet would have little leverage. The *why* was a bit more abstract: They believed that since the South had lost, it was obvious that God had decreed it would be so. Southern defenders rarely, if ever, asked themselves if perhaps they might have been in the wrong in some sense, and therefore God had not supported them. Instead they presumed that they could only have been right and therefore there must be some other reason why God had allowed the Confederates to lose. God had done it as a form of loving chastisement, and He had used the Yankee hordes to see to His will, as He had used the Babylonians or Assyrians against the Israelites in the Old Testament.

These two points came together to serve as the one sufficient explanation as to why a perfect general like Lee could still lose a war. First, Lee himself was flawless, at least in terms of military strategy and tactics. He simply could not get his bumbling subordinates to follow his orders as they should have. The fault, therefore, was theirs and not Lee's. Second, if God Himself had determined that the South would lose, what hope had Lee of victory? Lee emerged from the treatment as essentially perfect in every respect, a tragic figure who, despite his incredible abilities, was destined to fail.

Of course, there was some truth to this picture, and that was what made the scenario believable. Lee did indeed have problems with subordinates not obeying his orders, and several times that fact may have affected the outcome of battles. Longstreet's obtuse behavior no doubt undermined Lee's effectiveness at Gettysburg. Did this lessen Lee's responsibility as commander? It did not, and it is unlikely that he would have thought so himself. After all, one significant reason why Lee had so much trouble with his subordinates what that he could not bring himself to confront them when necessary. As for the role God played, it is highly unlikely that anyone will know what, if anything, He had to do with Lee's defeat unless the opportunity permits itself to ask in person. In the absence of that, the Lee cult could say whatever it liked and leave people to make assumptions.

To these advocates of the Lost Cause, Lee came to embody everything that they wanted the war to be about. Lee was a reluctant slaveholder and clearly fought in the war in defense of states' rights. As time passed and more and more people wanted to insist that the war had nothing to do with slavery, they presented a selective depiction of Lee's writings on the issue. By carefully excluding some of his more damning quotations, they made Lee look like a tragic progressive figure who knew that slavery was dying in the South. He therefore took up his sword in defense of his state alone. Lee, then, was the personification of an unjust war that resulted in the debasement of a superior society by an inferior one.

Gradually, Lee became the foremost hero of the South, but by the late 1800s he still was not a national phenomenon. Initially, he had been reviled in the North, and he had been circumspect about visiting his friends there for fear that he would damage their reputations. Over the course of the next 40 years, as the aging veterans looked back with nostalgia to the war, both sections of the country began to see Lee as the foremost example of what the South had stood and fought for. Many even began to lament the fact that the North had won, thereby extinguishing *antebellum* Southern culture. The reality of slavery was downplayed, and the idea of Southern chivalry and decorum exalted. This trend was aided by an increased Southern literary output. Dozens of articles, novels, and works of history came out, glorifying the Old South and by extension Lee himself. Lee became one of the first nominees for the new American Hall of Fame, and both presidents Theodore Roosevelt and Woodrow Wilson praised him as one of the leading Americans in history. He was a central feature of the various celebrations for the 60th and 75th anniversaries of the war. People all over the country had simply stopped thinking of Lee as human and instead saw him as a symbol.

The final major push came once again from Virginia. Douglas Southall Freeman was the editor of the Richmond *News Leader* and in 1934 he published his monumental study of Lee. In four well-written, thick volumes Freeman added the trappings of scholarship and research to Lee's legend. His biography, the result of 19 years of research, was originally expected to sell 4,000 copies—it sold well over 35,000 and became for years the definitive work on Lee. While Freeman did not maintain that Lee was perfect, he still cloaked him in such a drape of noble, tragic glory that much of the mystique that had accumulated around Lee became permanent. Freeman himself became entrenched as virtually the only author on Lee to matter, and many pundits did not think there would be anything more to say about Lee after Freeman.

More authors did come, and in many ways they provided the counter point to the "Lee as a god" school of history. Newer authors such as Emory Thomas and Thomas Connelly began to re-examine Lee as a human being and his previous biographers as a phenomenon in and of themselves. They focused as much on Lee's failures as on his successes, and they certainly did not accept his divine status. That trend has continued through to the modern day, and includes the present effort. While some historians have perhaps gone too far in their attempt to show Lee's foibles, pushing their claims past what reasonable historical evidence can support, much progress has been made in restoring the sense of realism and balance that Lee himself would have liked to see in his legacy.

This does not mean, however, that Lee has lost the mystique he accumulated over the course of the years. Many diehard believers still essentially worship Lee, and place all criticism of him out of bounds. In historical reenactment circuits, he remains a superstar, and tens of thousands of people still flock to the battlefield at Gettysburg each year to emotionally speculate on what might have been. Lee memorabilia makes millions of dollars a year. Even many serious scholars of the war still regard Lee with a sense of awe.

In the end of it all, what are we to make of Robert Lee? Lee was simply a human being, though a very distinguished one. Lee accomplished some amazing feats in his lifetime, and throughout it all he maintained a strong personal character and a sense of honor that was as beyond reproach as could be expected from any real, living, breathing person. That in itself gives him a serious claim to history's attention, and the fact that he was not a god simply makes his example more meaningful. If Lee was human, then we have something we can learn from him.

SELECTED BIBLIOGRAPHY

BOOKS

Carmichael, Peter S. *Audacity Personified: The Generalship of Robert E. Lee*. Baton Rouge: University of Louisiana Press, 2004.

Connelly, Thomas. *The Marble Man: Robert E. Lee and His Image in American Society*. New York: Knopf, 1977.

Davis, Burke. *Gray Fox: Robert E. Lee and the Civil War*. New York: Holt, Rinehart and Winston, 1956.

Dowdey, Clifford. *Lee: A Biography*. Boston: Little, Brown, 1965.

Dowdey, Clifford. *Lee's Last Campaign*. Boston: Little, Brown, 1960.

Dowdey, Clifford. *The Seven Days: The Emergence of Lee*. New York: Fairfax Press, 1978.

Fellman, Michael. *The Making of Robert E. Lee*. Baltimore: Johns Hopkins University Press, 2000.

Fishwick, Marshall. *Lee after the War*. New York: Dodd, Mead, 1963.

Flood, Charles B. *Lee: The Last Years*. Boston: Houghton Mifflin, 1981.

Forehand, Thomas, Jr. *Lee's Lighter Side*. Gretna, LA: Pelican Publishing, 2006.

Freeman, Douglas Southall. *R. E. Lee*. New York: Touchstone, 1991.

Fuller, J.F.C. *Grant and Lee: A Study in Personality*. Bloomington: Indiana University Press, 1957.

Gallagher, Gary. *Lee and His Army in Confederate History*. Chapel Hill: University of North Carolina Press, 2001.

Gallagher, Gary. *Lee and His Generals in War and Memory*. Baton Rouge: Louisiana State University Press, 1998.

Gallagher, Gary. *Lee the Soldier*. Lincoln: University of Nebraska Press, 1996.

Harsh, Joseph L. *Confederate Tide Rising*. Kent, OH: Kent State University Press, 1998.

Harsh, Joseph L. *Sounding the Shallows*. Kent, OH: Kent State University Press, 2000.

Harsh, Joseph L. *Taken at the Flood*. Kent, OH: Kent State University Press, 1999.

Lee, Fitzhugh. *General Lee*. New York: D. Appleton and Co., 1894.

Lee, Robert E. *Recollections and Letters of General Robert E. Lee*. Garden City, NY: Doubleday, 1960.

Lee, Robert E. *The Wartime Papers of Robert E. Lee*. Ed. Clifford Dowdey. Boston: Little, Brown, 1961.

Lee, Robert E., and Jefferson Davis. *Lee's Dispatches: The Unpublished Letters of General Robert. E. Lee*. New York: Putnam, 1957.

Marshall, Charles: *An Aide de Camp to Lee*. Boston: Little, Brown, 1927.

Maurice, Frederick. *Robert E. Lee: The Soldier*. Boston: Houghton Mifflin Co., 1925.

McCaslin, Richard. *Lee in the Shadow of Washington*. Baton Rouge: Louisiana State University Press, 2001.

Nolan, Alan T. *Lee Considered*. Chapel Hill: University of North Carolina Press, 1991.

Perry, John. *Lady of Arlington: Mrs. Robert E. Lee*. Sisters, OR: Multnomah Publishers, 2001.

Reid, Brian. *Robert E. Lee: An Icon for a Nation*. Amherst, NY: Prometheus Books, 2007.

Rister, Carl, *Robert E. Lee in Texas*. Norman: University of Oklahoma Press, 1946.

Taylor, Walter Herron. *Lee's Adjutant*. Columbia: University of South Carolina, 1995.

Thomas, Emory. *Robert E. Lee*. New York: W.W. Norton, 1995.

Woodworth, Steven E. *Davis and Lee at War*. Lawrence: University Press of Kansas, 1995.

Woodworth, Steven E. *Jefferson Davis and His Generals*. Lawrence: University Press of Kansas, 1990.

ONLINE RESOURCES

Biography

Answers.com Robert E. Lee Topic Collection. http://www.answers.com/topic/robert-e-lee

Blount, Roy Jr. "Making Sense of Robert E. Lee." *Smithsonian Magazine* (July 2003). http://www.smithsonianmag.com/history-archaeology/robertlee.html

Brasington, Larry Jr. "Robert E. Lee (1-19-1807 / 10-12-1870): Beloved General of the South." 2010. From Revolution to Reconstruction. http://www.let.rug.nl/usa/B/relee/relee.htm

Danforth, Courtney, Alex Lesman, and American Studies @ UVA. "The Apotheosis of Robert E. Lee." American Studies at UVA. http://xroads.virginia.edu/~cap/lee/lee.html

Dowdey, Clifford. "Robert E. Lee." In *Britannica Encyclopedia*. Britannica Online Encyclopedia. 2011. http://www.britannica.com/EBchecked/topic/334566/Robert-E-Lee

Dugdale-Pointon, T. "General Robert E. Lee (1807–70)." Military History Encyclopedia on the Web. http://www.historyofwar.org/articles/people_lee_robert.html

Freeman, Douglas Southall. *R. E. Lee: A Biography. New York and London: Charles Scribner's Sons, 1934.* http://penelope.uchicago.edu/Thayer/E/Gazetteer/People/Robert_E_Lee/FREREL/home.html

Hamilton, J.G. De Roulhac and Mary Thompson Hamilton. *The Life of Robert E. Lee For Boys and Girls*. Boston and New York: Houghton Mifflin Company, 1917. Washington and Lee University. http://leearchive.wlu.edu/?page=reference/books/hamilton/index.html

Heiser, John. "Biography of General Robert E. Lee." September 1998. National Park Service: Gettysburg National Military Park. http://www.nps.gov/gett/historyculture/people.htm

Jones, Mark. "Robert Edward Lee." January 21, 2002. National Park Service: Arlington House. http://www.nps.gov/arho/historyculture/robert-lee.htm

New York Times Topics: Robert E. Lee. http://www.nytimes.com/info/robert-e-lee/

Pryor, Elizabeth Brown. "Robert Edward Lee (ca. 1806–1870)." *Encyclopedia Virginia* (2009). http://encyclopediavirginia.org/Lee_Robert_Edward_1807-1870

Public Broadcasting Service. "Biography: Robert E. Lee." American Experience. Public Broadcasting Service Website. http://www.pbs.org/wgbh/americanexperience/features/biography/grant-lee/

Sifakis, Stewart. "General Robert E. Lee." Who Was Who In the Civil War? http://www.americancivilwarhistory.org/generalrobertelee historyandbiography.html

Stewart, Richard W., ed. "Chapter 12: The Civil War, 1864–1865." *American Military History Vol. 1: The United States Army and the Forging of a Nation*, 1175–1917. http://www.history.army.mil/books/amh-v1/ch12.htm

Stratford Hall. "General Robert E. Lee." 2005–2011. Stratford Hall Association. http://www.stratfordhall.org/learn/lees/robert_e_lee.php

Virginia Historical Society. Publications. History Notes. History Corner. "Lee After the War." http://www.vahistorical.org/publications/historycorner_lee.htm

Primary Source Collections

Battles and Leaders of the Civil War. http://ehistory.osu.edu/osu/books/battles/index.cfm

The Civil War Home Page, 1997–2009. http://www.civil-war.net/

Civil War Trust. Education. History. Civil War Primary Sources. 2011. http://www.civilwar.org/education/history/primarysources/

The Official Records of the Wars of the Rebellion. http://www.civilwarhome.com/records.htm

The Robert E. Lee Papers at Washington and Lee University. http://miley.wlu.edu/LeePapers/

Robert E. Lee Quotes from BrainyQuote. http://www.brainyquote.com/quotes/authors/r/robert_e_lee.html

Timelines

National Park Service Timeline. http://www.nps.gov/museum/exhibits/arho/Robert_E_LEEchronology.pdf

Stratford Hall Official Site. http://www.stratfordhall.org/learn/lees/relchrono.php

Timelines.com. http://timelines.com/topics/robert-e-lee

Today in Civil War History. http://www.todayincivilwarhistory.com/lee.php

INDEX

About the Author

BRIAN C. MELTON, Ph.D., is currently an associate professor of history at Liberty University in Lynchburg, Virginia. He has also published a study of the life of Union general Henry W. Slocum.